The Political Theology of Kierkegaard

New Perspectives in Ontology
Series Editors: Peter Gratton, Southeastern Louisiana University, and
Sean J. McGrath, Memorial University of Newfoundland, Canada

Publishes the best new work on the question of being and the history of metaphysics

After the linguistic and structuralist turn of the twentieth century, a renaissance in metaphysics and ontology is occurring. Following in the wake of speculative realism and new materialism, this series aims to build on this renewed interest in perennial metaphysical questions, while opening up avenues of investigation long assumed to be closed. Working within the Continental tradition without being confined by it, the books in this series will move beyond the linguistic turn and rethink the oldest questions in a contemporary context. They will challenge old prejudices while drawing upon the speculative turn in post-Heideggerian ontology, the philosophy of nature and the philosophy of religion.

Editorial Advisory Board
Thomas J. J. Altizer, Maurizio Farraris, Paul Franks, Iain Hamilton Grant, Garth Green, Adrian Johnston, Catherine Malabou, Jeff Malpas, Marie-Eve Morin, Jeffrey Reid, Susan Ruddick, Michael Schulz, Hasana Sharp, Alison Stone, Peter Trawny, Uwe Voigt, Jason Wirth, Günter Zöller

Books available
The Political Theology of Schelling, Saitya Brata Das
Continental Realism and its Discontents, edited by Marie-Eve Morin
The Contingency of Necessity: Reason and God as Matters of Fact, Tyler Tritten
The Problem of Nature in Hegel's Final System, Wes Furlotte
Schelling's Naturalism: Motion, Space and the Volition of Thought, Ben Woodard
Thinking Nature: An Essay in Negative Ecology, Sean J. McGrath
Heidegger's Ontology of Events, James Bahoh
The Political Theology of Kierkegaard, Saitya Brata Das
The 1801 Schelling–Eschenmayer Controversy: Nature and Identity, Benjamin Berger and Daniel Whistler

Books forthcoming
The Late Schelling and the End of Christianity, Sean J. McGrath
Schelling's Ontology of Powers, Charlotte Alderwick
Hölderlin's Philosophy of Nature, edited by Rochelle Tobias
Affect and Attention in Deleuze and Whitehead: Ecological Attunement, Russel J. Duvernoy

www.edinburghuniversitypress.com/series/epnpio

The Political Theology of Kierkegaard

SAITYA BRATA DAS

EDINBURGH
University Press

Edinburgh University Press is one of the leading university presses in the UK. We publish academic books and journals in our selected subject areas across the humanities and social sciences, combining cutting-edge scholarship with high editorial and production values to produce academic works of lasting importance. For more information visit our website: edinburghuniversitypress.com

© Saitya Brata Das, 2020, 2022

Edinburgh University Press Ltd
The Tun – Holyrood Road,
12(2f) Jackson's Entry,
Edinburgh EH8 8PJ

First published in hardback by Edinburgh University Press 2020

Typeset in 11/13 Adobe Garamond by
Servis Filmsetting Ltd, Stockport, Cheshire

A CIP record for this book is available from the British Library

ISBN 978 1 4744 7413 9 (hardback)
ISBN 978 1 4744 7414 6 (paperback)
ISBN 978 1 4744 7415 3 (webready PDF)
ISBN 978 1 4744 7416 0 (epub)

The right of Saitya Brata Das to be identified as the author of this work has been asserted in accordance with the Copyright, Designs and Patents Act 1988, and the Copyright and Related Rights Regulations 2003 (SI No. 2498).

Contents

Acknowledgements	vii
Introduction	1
1 Spectres of Schelling	17
2 Event and Existence	35
3 Conflagration	75
4 Sovereign Love	107
Bibliography	131
Names Index	135
Subject Index	137

Acknowledgements

Once again it is a joyous thanks-giving occasion, the occasion to thank the very same unforgettable people in my life, and the same ones who made the publication of this book possible: Sean McGrath (to whom this little work of love is dedicated) and Peter Gratton, Carol Macdonald and her colleagues at Edinburgh University Press. Once again it is a joyous feast of love with Sarita, Mrinmay and Reyansh; an occasion to celebrate with my very dear brother Debabrata and my teacher-colleague-friend of a lifetime, Franson Manjali.

I have reused a few paragraphs from my earlier book *The Political Theology of Schelling* in the first chapter 'Spectres of Schelling'. I gratefully acknowledge Edinburgh University Press for permission to reuse them.

I am come to send fire on the earth; and what will I, if it be already kindled?
Luke (12:49)

So soon as the fourth estate comes into the picture it is possible to rule only in godly way, religiously. But to rule religiously, to be religiously the ruler, is to be the sufferer, ruling religiously is suffering.
Kierkegaard (*The Book of Adler*)

For

Sean McGrath

Theologian, philosopher, my eternal friend

Introduction

The closure of immanence

The epochal principle – the *arché* – of modernity that legitimates its fundamental projection can be indicated to be 'immanence' or 'autonomy'. It is not for nothing that this projection is arrived at negatively: immanence as release *from* . . ., or autonomy as freedom *from* all that is heteronymous, whether we call that heteronymous 'God' or 'nature'. The fundamental projection of modernity – its sovereign myth, if we can call it so – lies in its *auto-nomos*: the *self*-giving of the law, the *self*-grounding of its essential task and vocation which, in a famous essay on Enlightenment, Immanuel Kant calls 'coming to maturity' or 'adulthood' (Kant 1991: 54–60). If the language of 'myth' can be said to be basically 'auto-poesis', or 'auto-saying', then the epochal myth of modernity is nothing other than itself 'mythic' par excellence. The fundamental projection of modernity, its hegemonic fantasm, is the myth of autonomy – namely, the myth of 'Reason' – which is the myth par excellence.

Theodor Adorno and Max Horkheimer in their well-known book *Dialectic of Enlightenment* (Adorno and Horkheimer 2002) display the mythic constitution of the Enlightenment project which, negatively, determines itself as freedom *from* myth, replacing religion (which is confused with myth) with the purgative power of Reason. This paradox is the heart of the fundamental projection of modernity. The epochal condition of modernity, out of its fundamental mythic ground (which it calls 'rational' ground), attempts to liquidate the power of myth (what it considers as 'myth', namely, 'religion'): Reason is 'auto-*nomos*', while religion (which it calls 'myth') is the *nomos* of the other (other than 'human', namely: God or nature). Reason (the self-giving of reason, the-why or the ground), in the immanence of its self-presence, releases us from the bondage of transcendence (God or nature), from the cages of the divine law and from the cages of the law of nature. The de-mythologising projection of Reason that grounds itself on its own law is, thus, the mythic constitution par excellence: it consists of a new mode of legitimacy of the 'human' as that being who, now released from cages of the divine law and from the *nomos* of nature, comes to understand him-/herself as the sovereign master of his or her own destinal becoming. The stage of his/her self-becoming is neither to be determined by divine *nomos* nor on the stage of nature but to be understood as essentially *historical*. While the mythic (or religious) plane and the plane of nature are determined by the logic of transcendence, the realm of history – in its constantly progressive movement towards its perfection – is immanent in it: it is auto-generative and auto-constitutive. The 'human' can become perfect and can realise its utmost capacity and potentiality to-be only as 'the world-historical being'; as mere natural existence or as mere creaturely being created by God he or she is only this exposed, vulnerable and wounded being, non-autochthonous and non-aboriginal. Only as this 'world-historical being' whose logic of self-becoming is immanent in her/him, can s/he be autochthonous and aboriginal; only as the being who gives the law to itself – the very law of being – can that being be sovereign, being sovereign as to his own destiny. The logic of Reason – as reason-giving, as the principle of 'why', as the *arché* of giving-itself-ground (Heidegger 1998: 97–135) – is, thus, the very logic of legitimacy: the legitimacy of being 'human', the 'human' that has the *raison d'être* in oneself, and thus can alone be that being who is the sovereign on earth. The legitimacy of the human as this sovereign being can neither be deduced from the principle of nature nor from the principle out of religion but from the principle (*arché* – the why) which must be *the* principle par excellence: the principle of principles, the ultimate *arché*, the ultimate 'why' or the sovereign reason, namely, Reason itself: it is Reason alone that can legitimate all reasons and the very *raison d'être* of the being 'human'. This is why Reason alone is considered to be the sovereign principle – the *hegemonikon* – of the epochal condition of modernity: as self-giving-ground, Reason needs no transcendental condition for its very being. Reason is contemporaneous with itself, and has the potentiality in it to be coincident with itself: the logic of its self-becoming is immanent in it, for it always returns to the Same, like the voyage of Odyssey, constantly re-appropriating and recuperating what is heteronymous (nature or God) to it until the heterogeneous elements are completely permeated (in the triple sense of Hegelian *Aufhebung*: negation, preservation and elevation) by immanence. The metaphysical foundation of the epochal condition of modernity is certain monism of being: the monism of being where there will no longer be left any trace of hetero-genesis. The logic of sovereignty which constitutes the hegemony of modernity is inextricably linked with the monism of being. Its metaphysical violence lies in its attempt to create a certain type, shape or *figura* of being 'human' (ibid.: 291–322). The metaphysical violence of this *figuration*, of which technology is the most disclosing example at the limit of metaphysics, is thoughtfully brought to our attention by the works of Martin Heidegger (1997) and Hans Jonas (1985).

The violence of this metaphysics, or the metaphysical violence of *figuration* which lies in the immanentising projection of the modern hegemony, phenomenalises itself or makes itself most visible precisely at the moment when the fundamental principle of the hegemony withers away, or becomes 'epochal': 'regional, dated, finite and finished in both senses of the word: complete as well as terminated' (Schürmann 1986: 5). The *arché* of the modernity that elicits from us 'normative obligation' (Schürmann 2003) now becomes de-legitimate: Reason no longer serves as the principle of legitimacy of the hegemony of modernity.

At the epochal closure of modernity – the instance of closure being, at the same time, the very instance of opening – its fundamental projection (its immanentising projection) is exposed open to what is unthinkable for it: the event of transcendence *to come* which, as such, is the eschatological event par excellence. The closure of immanence is burst open, eschatologically, to what is not immanent in it, and what does not present itself in any immanence of self-presence: the un-enclosed *absconditus* that puts into question the claim of any sovereign figure on the worldly order on the metaphysical foundation of monism. That to which the world is burst open from its very ground is neither *this* worldly nor the *other* worldly event: the event of *eschaton* that arrives, out of the voiding of worldly attributes, is not, then, the intra-mundane event, whether from *this* or *that* side of the world; it is not the event *of* the world but *the event* of the world. As *event absconditus*, the *eschaton* does not belong to the totality of the worldly events, namely: it does not occur as event (datable, localisable, whether at the empirical or ideal level) on the plane of the world-historical politics where the figure of the human (as the being who gives himself the law of being), 'legitimately', is supposed to exist as the sovereign being on earth. How to think this radical transcendence which, unlike the transcendence that we know to be, is not a principle of legitimation, and which, as such, does not serve as the *arché* of any worldly hegemony? How to think of transcendence which is not a mere reversal of immanence, and thus not mere reduplication of the very same hegemonic order?: a radicalised transcendence must it be, outside of the opposition of 'transcendence' (as the principle of legitimation) and 'immanence', an opening to the radical exteriority whose absolute and irreducible heterogeneity opens up a void into the heart of the world! Not a truth *of* the world – neither of *this* nor of *that* world – the truth of transcendence must be an infinite paradox where paradox is the very indication of infinity: the glory is *kenosis*! An unbearable paradox it is, the unthought of the world, where oppositions coincide at the instance of *kenosis*: this paradox marks the very event of *eschaton* which opens up the world precisely at an un-pre-thinkable instance of its ending. In that sense, the 'end' is not 'the' end but also the beginning or inauguration par excellence (Moltmann 2004):

> King Oedipus has an eye many perhaps . . .
> Life is death and death is a kind of life. (Hölderlin 1966: 604–5)

Radicalising transcendence

To reintroduce transcendence, while radicalising it, is not to make it the ultimate and legitimizing *arché* of a new hegemony in turn that merely replaces the phantasm of immanence; the task is rather to deliver any *arché* of legitimation to its utter destitution. The paradox of the infinite, or the infinitude of the paradox – that glory is *kenosis*! – uncouples the *Koinon* that links transcendence to any *figuration* of sovereignty. The unthinkable plenitude or excess of transcendence whose excess is simultaneously an utter destitution: this paradox that *sets apart* and *separates* the world from its foundation (the eschatological event par excellence!) renders transcendence of the holy irreducible to any *figuration* of worldly sovereignty. Transcendence marks the arrival of the holy: the *apartness* of *the-that* which keeps open the world from its very foundation by an eschatological judgement in the name of justice; the holy comes out of the *Abgrund* by bursting open the world from its ground. Faith anticipates the arrival of the holy conflagration (the conflagration of the holy) that

> is separation (*Aussonderung*) and setting apart (*Absonderung*); being holy means being apart. The holy is the terror that shakes the foundations of the world. The shock caused by the holy bursts asunder the foundations of the world for salvation [das *Heil*]. It is the holy that passes judgement in the court of history. History exists only when truth is separated from error, when truth is illuminated from mystery. History is elucidated from the mystery of error to the revelation of truth. (Taubes 2009: 194)

The arrival of the holy, then, marks the eschatological suspension of the worldly *nomos*, and as such it is truly the event of exception: the advent of the holy *in-cepts* the realm of justice by an *ex-ception* – by *de-parting* and *a-parting* – from the law of the worldly being. The *advient* of the holy is the event of *distance* – a *distensio* – which the law of the worldly order can't measure, from which it *differs* and *defers* (Derrida 1984: 1–28) and is the *differend* par excellence. No principle of *analogia entis* can measure up the distance of the immeasurable – and the immeasurable distance – of *differend*, for they don't present themselves as 'entis' at all; they never come together on the synchrony of an immanence of self-presence. As such, the *advient* of *the holy* puts into question infinitely all possible theodicy of history, that is, all possible deification of the profane order of worldly *nomos*, or all possible attempt at incarnation of the divine at the level of world-historical politics. Therefore, the progress of humanity as the world-historical being (the being who gives law of his own being out of his autochthonous ground) on the stage of the world-historical politics does not any more represent or embody the consummation that is made possible by the eschatological advent of the holy. The holy, in all its apocalyptic paradox, that *sets apart* the world from its foundation, can't be realised by the world-historical humanity at the level of the world-historical politics, for the *advent* puts into question the very legitimacy of any worldly *figuration* at all! An infinite transcendence it remains, which can neither be proved nor disproved by any empirical-historical testimony, for its arrival is without fate or without destiny: an incalculable arrival, inaccessible to knowledge, un-programmable and un-anticipatable, it can't be confounded with the *telos* of the secularised theodicy of world-history. The eschatological consummation of history that refuses to be translated into the *telos* of the secularised theodicy of the world-historical politics is forever the event non-contemporaneous and non-coincident. It makes the time and the truth of the world destitute and desolate; a desolation that finds no consolation and salvation in the Absolute Concept realising itself on the worldly order of an anonymous totality, whether we name it as 'the state' or 'the Church'.

How to name this event of the absolute – which neither is the absolute figure of the state in the external order (the state) nor the absolute figure of the internal order (the Church) – if not the unconditional par excellence whose wisdom is foolishness and a scandal for the worldly being? Again it is the *para-doxa*: it presents its truth only as foolishness and its wisdom a scandal, and yet, it is precisely this weak and fragile truth, and this precarious wisdom – that knows no *figuration* into the form of a mythic or logical statement (by which to claim validity and legitimacy) – that brings to *kenosis* the power of the worldly sovereignties and the force of the worldly *nomos* : a paradox upon paradox which Søren Kierkegaard, whom we will be reading here, calls in his unique and singular manner 'absurd'. The absurd whose power is *impotentia*, whose wisdom is foolishness, whose truth is a scandal: here the light of our knowledge becomes dizzy with an excess, and turns into the abyss of the night; here de-cision (*decidere*: cutting through) *cuts through* the *nomos* of the worldly reason, and arrives by traversing a passage where knowledge fails, and where the act of deducing from the first principle (*arché*) comes to a sudden halt. The *de-cision* by the absurd is, then, a *wholly other* decision, not accomplished by the deducing act of knowledge: the *ratio* of Reason can't serve as its measure or as ground. The event of radical transcendence is neither a principle of knowledge nor a principle of action; it is not, in this sense, opposed to immanence (as principle). Opening to the radical exteriority, it makes absurd the monism of being. It is absurd in two senses of the term: it must appear absurd to the wisdom and truth of the world; second, it in turn makes any claims of worldly wisdom absurd. It is ridiculous, it is a hilarious absurdity; it provokes laughter and humour when any worldly sovereign figure claims sovereignty on a theological ground. The only sovereign on the worldly order of history is the martyr, and hence, is decisively the non-sovereign one. Hence is Kierkegaard's laughter which he throws each time he speaks of the terribly serious philosophy professor – the official hairdresser of the Prussian state – namely, G. W. F Hegel.

The logic of sovereignty

Carl Schmitt in his 1922 book called *Political Theology* (Schmitt 2005) formulated the concept of 'political theology' around the problematic of sovereignty. 'All significant concepts of the modern theory of the state', writes Schmitt,

> are secularized theological concepts not only because of their historical development – in which they were transferred from theology to the theory of the state, whereby, for example, the omnipotent God became the omnipotent lawgiver – but also because of their systematic structure, the recognition of which is necessary for a sociological consideration of these concepts. The exception in jurisprudence is analogous to the miracle in theology. Only by being aware of this analogy can we appreciate the manner in which the philosophical ideas of the state developed in the last centuries. (Ibid.: 36)

His concept of 'political theology' – and Heinrich Meier reminds us that he borrowed the term from Mikhail Bakunin's book called *The Political Theology of Mazzini* (Meier 2006: 75–88) – is founded upon the Catholic principle of *analogia entis*: who the God is in the divine realm is analogous to the worldly sovereign figure in the profane order; it is he who is the source of *auctoritus* who alone can decide 'on the state of exception'. What is, then, the state of exception – the state of exception on the concrete order of the political – according to Schmitt? And we know from Jacob Taubes that Schmitt is indeed the thinker of concrete actuality par excellence, unlike his interlocutor Hans Blumenberg who is the thinker of metaphor (Taubes 2003: 69).

'All law', according to Schmitt, 'is situational law'. 'Every general norm demands a normal, everyday frame of life to which it can be factually applied and which is subjected to its regulations. The norm requires a homogenous medium' (Schmitt 2005: 13). However, in a state of exception – for example, in situation of civil disorder irrupting from below (which Schmitt, in another book, personifies as the earth monster Behemoth) (Schmitt 2008b) – when the 'normal, everyday frame of mind' no longer exists for law is to be 'factually applied', the decision demands an 'auctoritus' who can only be a 'who' and not a 'what' (in an entirely different register Martin Heidegger in his *Being and Time* points out that Dasein is, each time, a 'who' and not a 'what'); the one who can decide on this state of exception, being himself an exception (who alone has the power to *declare* which is the situation of exception, and thus, has the power of decision). Let's not miss here the inextricable link between the speech act of declaration and the logic of sovereignty. It is this exception, so Schmitt argues, that 'cannot be subsumed' to the 'homogeneous medium' of the normative situation, and, precisely because of this, the exception can reveal 'most clearly the essence of the state's authority'; it discloses that 'to produce law it need not be based on law' (Schmitt 2005: 13).

Here is, then, the strange and paradoxical character of the exception: 'the norm is destroyed in exception' and yet, it remains 'accessible to jurisprudence' (ibid.: 12). This is because the sovereign, who alone is the *auctoritus* here (who alone has the power and 'legitimate right' to declare), can alone juristically (using a certain Article of the constitution) suspend the normative order of the law to bring a new order: the sovereign is, in a way, at once outside and inside the law. To bring forth a new order of law by a suspension of the given order of norms needs a force, the force of exception, which can't be explicated in the manner of the positivistic conception of the law according to which the state 'is a system of ascriptions to a last point of ascription and to a basic norm . . . the state is the terminal point of ascription, the point at which the ascriptions, which constitute the essence of juristic consideration, "can stop" . . . an uninterrupted system of orders, starting from the original, the ultimate, from the highest to a lower, meaning a delegated norm, can be conceived in such a fashion' (ibid.: 19). Hence the normative-positivistic conception of the law which thinks that the state is 'identical with its constitution, with the uniform basic norm' (ibid.), cannot serve as the explicative principle of the very emergence of the new order of the law out of a state of exception when 'law recedes' but 'the state remains' (ibid.: 12). The state of exception invalidates this identification of the state with its constitution. Thus the normative-positivistic conception of the law cannot explain the decision – and hence the paradoxical force of the sovereign – which has to be made (by whom if not by the sovereign?) on this state of exception when the law is suspended. Therefore, 'the exception can be more important to it than the rule . . . the exception is more interesting than the rule. The rule proves nothing; the exception proves everything: it confirms not only the rule but also its existence, which derives only from the exception' (ibid.: 15). From here follows a statement of Schmitt that is of decisive importance for us:

> A protestant theologian who demonstrated the vital intensity possible in theological reflection in the nineteenth century stated: 'the exception explains the general and itself. And if one wants to study the general correctly, one only needs to look around for a true exception. It reveals everything more clearly than does the general. If they cannot be explained, then the general also cannot be explained. The difficulty is usually not noticed because the general is not thought with passion but with a comfortable superficiality. The exception, on the other hand, thinks the general with intense passion.' (Ibid.)

Who is the Protestant theologian here who, without being named, is approvingly cited by the Catholic political theologian Carl Schmitt? The Protestant theologian is Søren Kierkegaard, and the citation is from his book *Repetition*. This Protestant theologian is the intellectual predecessor and intellectual authority for the Catholic Schmitt, the one who – like Schmitt himself – thinks with utmost passion the intensity of exception, and hence of the exception of decision: that the general does neither explain itself nor does the exception; it is the singular exception that alone explains, not only the general but also itself. The proximity that Schmitt approvingly discovers in the Protestant Kierkegaard (despite Kierkegaard being Protestant: this is important!) – lies in their common intellectual counterpart, their polemical target; namely, the pantheistic-immanent philosophy of history that finds such consummate expression in Hegel's theodicy of history.

Schmitt's political theology traces back all the evils of the contemporary society (the technology of politics in today's secular-liberal world of mass consumption, the neutralisation of politics in the name of 'objective', 'value free' truth, the totalisation of administrative rationality) to the secularising project of modernity whose most consummate expression is to be found in Hegelian pantheistic metaphysics of history:

> conceptions of transcendence will no longer be credible to most educated people, who will settle for either a more or less clear immanence-pantheism

or a positivist indifference toward any metaphysics. Insofar as it retains the concept of God, the immanence philosophy, which found its greatest systematic architect in Hegel, draws God into the world and permits law and the state to emanate from the immanence of the object . . .

If viewed from this perspective of the history of ideas, the development of the nineteenth century theory of the state displays two characteristic moments: the elimination of all theistic and transcendental conceptions and the formation of a new concept of legitimacy. The traditional principle of legitimacy obviously lost all validity. Neither the version of the Restoration based on private law and patrimony nor the one founded on a sentimental and reverent attachment was able to resist this development. Since 1848 the theory of public law has become 'positive', and behind this word is usually hidden its dilemma; or the theory has propounded in different paraphrases the idea that all power resides in the *pouvoir constituant* of the people, which means that the democratic notion of legitimacy has replaced the monarchical. (Ibid.: 50–1)

At stake here is the question of legitimacy: with the loss of authority (as a result of the liquidation of the established order of religion in modernity), legitimation of the sovereign power is in crisis, which Schmitt here laments. Against such a state of affairs, Schmitt constructs a political theology of apocalypticism that has nothing to do with suspension of the worldly hegemonies but rather to do with securing a place for the sovereign power who, being *Katechon* (Schmitt 2006: 59–61) restrains chaos rising from below. Despite being 'Protestant', Kierkegaard is for Schmitt the apocalyptic thinker of decision and exception par excellence who offers, at the epochal closure of modernity, the decisive critique of the secularising project of historical Reason. Schmitt, then, finds in this Protestant critique of the secularising liquidation and neutralisation of politics elements of his own political theology which (Schmitt's), as we now know, is based upon the notion of sovereignty.

We have seen that Schmitt's notion of sovereignty ('Sovereign is he who decides on the exception' (Schmitt 2005: 5)) is based on the (Catholic) theological concept of *analogia entis*. The apocalyptic intensity of decision is the prerogative of the sovereign figure who, as the power 'to suspend valid law', is true *auctoritus* ('Because the authority to suspend valid law . . . is so much the actual mark of sovereignty' (ibid.: 9)): for Schmitt, this possibility of *auctoritus* ('to suspend valid law') must invoke the very power of the myth ('to great politics belongs the "arcanum"') (Schmitt 1996: 34). The apocalyptic intensity of exception and decision, in Schmitt's counter-revolutionary political theology, turns into the figure of sovereignty who is the very locus of *auctoritus*, and who alone can suspend the general order of legality to bring forth an entire new order of *nomos*: exception here, as Benjamin reminds us, turns demonic by becoming the rule (Benjamin

1985: 245–55) against which Benjamin thinks of a messianic exception without sovereignty, exception that suspends the *nomos* of the worldly without founding a new earthly hegemonic order in turn (Benjamin 1986: 312–13). It is, thus, not surprising that, for Schmitt, the dictator has remained the paradigmatic example of the sovereign figure who, as the true *Katechon*, restrains the chaos rising from below that threatens to destroy the state: in this manner, Schmittean *Katechon* becomes the real *raison d'état*, the ultimate *arché* of earthly hegemonies, the principle of justification and legitimation of worldly sovereignties eliciting from us 'normative obligations' (Schürmann 2003).

Secularisation of the eschatological

We have seen that it is against the Hegelian pantheistic-immanent metaphysics of history that both the 'Protestant theologian' Søren Kierkegaard and the political theologian Carl Schmitt – in two entirely different registers of thought and for two entirely different reasons (we will see how) – think of the transcendence of exception (or, the exception of transcendence). Here lies the proximity between the 'Protestant theologian' and the political theologian, and here too lies – and to show this is the very task of this work – their greatest distance. For the political theologian Schmitt, the exception is drawn on the figure of the sovereign (Schmitt draws the idea of *Kathekon* from St Paul's epistle (2 Thessalonians 2: 6–7)), whereas the 'Protestant theologian' Søren Kierkegaard draws the very idea of exception, which is the paradox of infinity, from the Pauline conception of *kenosis* (Philippians 2: 7): both conceptions occur in Pauline discourse in eschatological contexts. It is against the same secularised metaphysics of the history of Hegel that Kierkegaard formulates his eschatological vision of history, and Carl Schmitt formulates his 'political theology' as 'apocalyptic counter-revolutionary' thought, inspired by de Maistre, Donoso Cortés and de Bonald (Taubes 2013), and yet with entirely two different results. This proximity (also distance) explains Schmitt's quotation from Kierkegaard.

The idea of 'political theology' prophetically announces the decisive crisis of the self-legitimising project of modernity which, as we know from Karl Löwith, is nothing other than the secularisation of the Judeo-Christian 'eschatological pattern' of history (Löwith 1957: 2). In contrast to the Greek conception of history, whose fundamental principle is 'verification of prognostications concerning historiconatural event' (ibid.: 9), the philosophy of history opens up 'the temporal horizon for a final goal', 'an eschatological future' which 'exists for us only by expectation and hope' (ibid.: 6):

> The Christian and post-Christian outlook on history is futuristic, perverting the classical meaning of *historein*, which is related to present and past events. In the Greek and Roman mythologies and genealogies the past is re-presented as an everlasting foundation. In the Hebrew and Christian view of history the past is a promise to the future; consequently, the interpretation of the past becomes a prophecy in reverse, demonstrating the past as a meaningful 'preparation' for the future. Greek philosophers and historian were convinced that whatever is to happen will be on the same pattern and character as past and present events; they never indulged in the prospective possibilities of the future. (Ibid.)

Löwith goes on to say further:

> The Greek historians wrote pragmatic history centred around a great political event; the Church Fathers developed from Hebrew prophecy and Christian eschatology a theology of history focused on the supra-historical events of creation, incarnation, and consummation; the moderns elaborate a philosophy of history by secularizing theological principles and applying them to an ever increasing number of empirical facts. It seems as if the two great conceptions of antiquity and Christianity, cyclic motion and eschatological direction, have exhausted the basic approaches to the understanding of history. (Ibid.: 19)

In Hegel's 'philosophy of history', the secularisation of the 'eschatological pattern' assumes the form and movement of pantheistic metaphysics. Here again the eruption of Christ on the stage of history is the paradigm but it is now invested with speculative meaning (Löwith 1991): through Christ's death, there takes places the 'reconciliation' or 'mediation' (the dialectical 'synthesis': this dialectical concept of 'mediation' is precisely the target of Kierkegaard's eschatological critique) of the infinite (God) and the finite (the world) in a movement of the self-cancellation of negativity (*Aufhebung*), in a purely immanent manner, needing no transcendental outside as 'foundation' and 'ground'. In the Hegelian 'philosophy of history' (Löwith reminds us that this term is derived from Voltaire), which follows the eschatological pattern of Biblical thought but attempts to realise the Kingdom of God on the immanent plane of 'universal world history', the self-legitimising task of modernity (which is the meaning of *saeculum*) needs no 'outside': the order of *saeculum* bears within itself, in the immanence of self-presence, the prerogative of the eschatological judgement, now grasped as the *telos* of a triumphal march of the universal world-historical politics. The result is evident: Hegel's apology of the world finds objective expression when he deifies the modern state of Prussia as the very figure of the absolute in an objective manner (Hegel 1900: 16). The self-legitimising task of modernity, precisely in its mere taking up of the eschatological pattern, neutralises or liquidates the apocalyptic thorn, the poisonous sting of eschatological judgement that, in biblical discourses, judges the course of the worldly regimes and puts into question all earthly sovereignties. By taking away the apocalyptic sting of early Christianity,

> Hegel believes that, as a Christian Philosopher, he can answer this question by secularizing the Christian doctrine of providence and converting the salvation story of Christianity into a secular theodicy, for which the divine spirit is immanent in the world, the state is an earthly god and all history is divine. (Löwith 1991: 216)

Formulating a question

The Kierkegaardian eschatological notion of transcendence as much as the Schmittean 'apocalyptic counter-revolutionary' theologico-political notion of transcendence is built up against the Hegelian pantheistic-immanent metaphysics of history. This proximity has led Schmitt to find in Kierkegaard the apocalyptic thinker of decision and exception who offers, at the epochal closure of modernity, the decisive critique of the secularising project of historical Reason. Schmitt, then, finds in this Protestant critique of the secularising liquidation and neutralisation of politics elements of his own political theology that is chiefly concerned with the legitimation of the sovereign power on a theological foundation.

In this work I take up to examine, once again, the Kierkegaardian notions of 'decision' and 'exception' to show that they cannot be understood in Schmittean terms. Kierkegaard thinks transcendence eschatologically as the event that incalculably erupts in the midst of history, and tears asunder its immanence: here the event of *eschaton* is thought neither on the basis of the infinitely long temporal scale of progress nor as the Kingdom of God on earth as the *telos* of universal world-history, but in an 'impossible' and 'paradoxical' manner, in the spirit of early Christianity, and bypassing thereby 1,800 years of Christendom: it is the absolute event that, despite centuries of Christendom, leaves itself as remnant or trace of the void it has opened up, once and for all, at the very heart of time and at the very heart of the world, and keeping itself sheltered as eschatological promise for the justice *to come*. This absolute exteriority of the world, without itself being or becoming another 'world' in turn (and which hence is irreducible and inaccessible to all Christendom for all the time to come), is not, then, the event *in* time and *in* history: it does not, and it has not, occurred in any immanence of self-presence. In this sense, this breakthrough of eternity, the event par excellence, that vertically interrupts – and keeps on disrupting – the homogeneous march of world-historical progress, is the true 'origin' which can, at best, be paradox par excellence: there the impossible happens as impossible, the inapparent advents as the inapparent, de-formalising the constituted order of *nomos*. Kierkegaard calls it being 'contemporaneous' which is also, paradoxically, non-contemporaneous with all events that take place in any historical time of self-presence: the contemporaneity, while being non-contemporaneous with all that happens on the stage of world-historical triumphal politics, is the event of tearing – or, the wounding – that Kierkegaard would call something like 'infinite negativity' which no concept, not even Hegelian Concept of the concept, and no knowledge, not even Absolute Knowledge, will be able to measure. As impossible event, or as the event of the impossible, it is death (hence it evokes fear and trembling), but as the releasement from the order of *nomos* (for the law as death) it is also 'a kind of life' for us (as in Hölderlin and Heraclitus, as this event 'life is death and death is a kind of life'). Life, which is no longer *mere* life – and we know from Walter Benjamin that it is this mere life that the mythic violence of the law strikes (Benjamin 1986: 277–300), appears at this extreme limit of the possible (a kind of death) as alone that is redemptive.

How to think this paradox where opposites coincide at the blinding and dizzying instance of arrest, and where the moment is no longer a point on the scale of a time teleologically oriented but the sudden and momentary apparition of eternity, 'an atom of eternity'(Kierkegaard 1957: 79), if not as the exception without sovereignty? It is this exception, but without sovereignty, which calls forth a political theology that is based not upon any (Schmittean) *analogia entis* but upon the thought of the tearing apart and setting apart of the holy.

It is against the political theology of legitimation of the (earthly) sovereign power that Jacob Taubes evokes a 'negative political theology', a political theology from below: 'Carl Schmitt thinks apocalyptically, but from above, from the powers that be; I think from the bottom up' (Taubes 2013: 13). Against the apocalyptic counter-revolutionary political theology (ibid.: 1–18) of Schmitt which is inspired by counter-revolutionary philosophers of the state such as de Maistre, de Bonald and Donoso Cortés, Taubes invokes the political theology of exception without sovereignty, taking seriously into account the Pauline paradoxical messianic logic of *Verbund* ('covenant') which is free not only from ethnic ties but also from the earthly *nomos* of the Roman empire (Taubes 2003). In the spirit of Taubes's negative political theology, I attempt to think here, with the help of Kierkegaard, an exception without sovereignty. Such exception, far from enabling and legitimising the 'state' of sovereignty, rather makes impossible any claims on the part of earthly sovereign power in the profane order to legitimise itself by an appeal to theological foundation. This demands deconstruction of the theologico-political doctrine of *analogia entis* which is the theological basis of Schmitt's political claim.

Taking up some of Kierkegaard's later polemical writings, I attempt to show that at the heart of Kierkegaard's 'Christianity without Christendom' lies the idea of the gift that demands from us unconditional abandonment of all worldly sovereign powers and earthly glory. The very gift of being, eschatologically thought, demands that the worldly order must be emptied (*kenosis*) of all sovereignty. One can't miss here even the possibility of naming it as 'theological politics', if that comes to mean a certain theological delegitimation of politics where the very sense of 'the theological' itself would need rethinking and revision. I think it is not impossible, though it is difficult, if one takes Kierkegaardian thought to its radical consequences, passing via the Lutheran *destructio* (which makes 'the two kingdoms' as irreducible and incommensurable, and thereby empties out, kenotically, any possibility of sovereignty on the basis of the theologico-political principle of 'analogia'). It is the task of this work to show that in Kierkegaardian *destructio*, that radically puts into question not only the legitimising *arché* of immanence (as in the Hegelian pantheistic theodicy of history) but also the legitimising *arché* of transcendence (as in Schmittean political theology of sovereignty), there is at work the Lutheran *destructio* that passes onto Kierkegaard via the Schellingian kenotic eschatology of 'actuality without potentiality'. It is here we find, in a far more intense and explicit manner than in Schelling, the elements of a negative political theology of exception without sovereignty. I hope to show this through an exposition of his later polemical writings where 'Christianity without Christendom' (the latter being eighteen centuries old) is itself understood as a polemical (Kierkegaard calls it 'incendiary') event on the stage of history: a *stasis* (Peterson 2011: 68–105; Schmitt 2008a) or insurrection on the stage of history. Christianity, in the spirit of the one dying on the cross, and in the spirit of the apostles, is the *polemical* concept par excellence; its import lies in its negation or *nihilation* of worldly *potestas* on the cross, not by means of force but by an absolute abandonment ('My God, my God, Why hast thou abandoned me?').

This work renews the task, which I have formulated in my previous work on Schelling, to think of a political theology of exception that weakens sovereignties and makes destitute worldly hegemonies. This demands that we put forward an infinite critique of historical Reason – which is provided in such a powerful way by Søren Kierkegaard – along with a tireless deconstruction of the theologico-political principle of *analogia entis*. In his inimitable and original way Kierkegaard makes destitute the fundamental *arché* of the hegemony of modernity and opens for us the task for the new millennium to think without *arché*; that means, without hegemonies. By reintroducing the notion of transcendence, and yet by radicalising it (that is, not as mere opposed to or replacing immanence as another legitimising *arché*), I attempt to show here that like Schelling whose works he knew, Kierkegaard is the thinker of transcendence par excellence where at stake is nothing other than 'delegitimation', not only of political sovereign power on a theological foundation but of the very place of 'the human' as the sovereign being on the stage of world-historical politics. Kierkegaard thereby make destitute the hegemonic fantasm of modernity – the autonomy and sovereignty of the Subject – to introduce a new singularity ('that single individual') to come, thereby breaking away from the modern *hegemon-ikon* of the Subject.

Chapter 1

Spectres of Schelling

We know that Kierkegaard attended Schelling's much publicised lectures in Berlin on 'positive philosophy'. After listening to the second lecture, Kierkegaard writes:

> I am so happy to have heard Schelling's second lecture – indescribably. I have been pining and thinking mournful thoughts long enough. The embryonic child of thought leapt for joy within me, as in Elizabeth when he mentioned the word 'actuality' in connection with the relation of philosophy to actuality. I remember almost every word he said after that. Here, perhaps, clarity can be achieved. This one word recalled all my philosophical pains and sufferings. – And so that she, too, might share my joy. How willingly I would return to her, how eagerly I would coax myself to believe that this is the right course. – Oh, if only I could! – Now I have put all my hope in Schelling. (Kierkegaard 1909–1948: *JP* V 5535, Pap. III A 179)

Though Kierkegaard grew progressively disappointed with Schelling subsequently, the spectre of the later Schellingian thought – that is, the irreducible actuality of existence as the event without potentiality – has remained the haunting presence (that is, presence-in-absence, like a spectre) in Kierkegaardian thought. The later Kierkegaardian theologico-political 'deconstruction' of the logic of sovereignty, passing via his deconstruction of Hegelian theodicy of history and the Hegelian onto-theo-logic, cannot be fully appreciated and understood without taking into account the Schellingian eschatology of 'actuality without potentiality'. This consists of the more or less implicit presence of the later Schellingian attempt, in Kierkegaardian thought, to release the question of faith and Christianity from the grasp (*greifen*) of the concept (*Begriff*): the concept, the Concept of the concept (the Absolute Concept) being nothing other than the 'onto' and 'logical' grounding of the secularised theodicy of history, the concept serving as the 'ground' (the-why) or (self) grounding (therefore, immanent) labour of history: this is why Hegel could understand the concept itself as 'the seriousness, the suffering and the labour of the negative' (Hegel 1977: 10).

Therefore, to properly understand the Kierkegaardian eschatological deconstruction of 'Christendom', it is necessary to heed to 'the turning point' – *Kehre* – which precisely is the thought of the 'actuality without potentiality': this turning point is the point of an *exit* – from the onto-theological constitution of metaphysics – as much as a new inauguration 'outside metaphysics'; it is that of the 'instance' (*Augenblick*), of the abyss or caesura, where something other than the Absolute (understood as the self-grounding immanence of the concept) announces itself; that is: the actuality of the event, or the event of actuality (where what follows the 'of' does not represent a predicate) that interrupts and disrupts, eschatologically, the immanent plane of any theodicy of history. The transcendence of the heterogeneous is that of a plenitude which is 'touched' precisely at the unutterable instance of utter destitution of the worldly existence: this paradox does not occur in any figure on the secularised stage of world-historical politics. To bring this paradox to the notice of the young philosopher Søren Kierkegaard (who must follow his own 'way' to the point of denial of any allegiance to Schelling) and this very denial on his (Kierkegaard's) part of any decisive influence of Schelling on him, shows the spectral presence of Schellingian thought of the event on Kierkegaard's eschatological politics. For what manifests itself at 'this' point as this 'point' – which we see is an abyss – is not so much 'Schelling' as this individual name, or as this particular philosopher, but the very 'turning' itself, of/ from metaphysics, to a different, not yet named, 'destination'. 'Schelling' is, in that sense, 'the name' of the 'opening', by a paradoxical manner of 'exit' (*Ausgang*) to the advent of the event; it is the name of an 'exposure' to the wound of transcendence that demands for its arrival the twofold *conflagration* of the world and its *abandonment*/destitution. Both Schelling and Kierkegaard are concerned with the twofold – that of *conflagration* and *abandonment* – as the very task of thinking which, unconditionally, announces itself as *existential*: an unconditional demand, the claim of the unconditioned, in the name of which – whether one calls it Justice or Love – the realm of the conditioned negotiations of forces, of powers, of the law of the worldly with all its finite institutions is to be 'deconstructed'; that is: to be *released-open* by *giving-up* (in Eckhartian-Schellingian-Heideggerian double senses of *Gelassenheit*). While Hegel makes Absolute Knowledge the *telos* of his theodicy of history which in turn embodies itself in the objective order of world-historical politics (the modern state of Prussia), both Schellingian and Kierkegaardian kenotic eschatology make Love as the eschatological advent of the holy out of the groundlessness of divine freedom and decision which, while putting into question any figure of the absolute in profane history, remains itself 'undeconstructable': it is the unconditional Love that makes the law of the worldly inoperative and workless. In Schellingian words, Love is the emptying of potentiality. As such, this exception – this unconditional Love – does not follow the logic of sovereignty; it is not conditioned upon the non-identification of the law and the state. While the latter – the non-identification of the law and the state – still belongs to the juristic order (as in Carl Schmitt's political theology), the exception of Love is exception even to the non-identification of the law and the state. In that sense, this non-sovereign exception – of the unconditioned Love – is only truly sovereign exception: it is exception even to sovereignty.

While both Schelling and Kierkegaard think the unconditioned Love in Christian (Protestant) manner in which Love unconditionally is opened up in faith in absolute heterogeneity to the institutional order of the law, their 'deconstructions' are decisively influenced by one and the same pagan philosopher: Socrates, the master of irony. It is this influence that sets the Nietzschean Dionysian tragic philosophy apart from Schellingian and Kierkegaardian political theologies, not to speak of the more obvious trait: that unlike Nietzschean (and also Marxist) deconstruction of Hegelian theodicy of history that is carried out in a non-Christian and 'atheistic' manner (if it can still be called 'atheism'),[1] both Schellingian 'positive philosophy' of revelation and Kierkegaardian 'Christianity without Christendom' are carried out in decisively religious-Christian manners. While Nietzsche looks ahead of Socrates and wants to look 'beyond' him to the pre-Socratic thinkers (Heraclitus) – thus, for Nietzsche, the Heraclitean tragic thought remains unthinkable in the history of Occidental metaphysics – both Schelling and Kierkegaard see Socrates as the decisive figure, second only to Christ. It is Schelling especially – the early Schelling – who can be called the Platonist thinker par excellence (or, Socratic thinker, Socrates as we know from Plato), and he sets his thought, paradoxically, against the Neo-Platonic Plotinus. The Platonist against the Neo-Platonist: this seems to describe the early Schelling rather well. Similarly, Socrates is the decisively important philosopher for the young Kierkegaard as his doctoral dissertation amply illustrates.

Differing from Nietzsche's and Marx's 'atheistic' eschatological deconstruction of Christianity, both Schellingian and Kierkegaardian Christian eschatologies without 'Christendom' can perhaps be called 'immanent' deconstruction: it is the task of thinking Christianity in its entire apocalyptic sting, turning up against 'Christendom' of 1,800 years, and thereby refusing to participate in the secularising project of modernity. On the other hand, Nietzsche's and Marx's eschatologies can be called 'immanent' for an entirely different reason: their task is that of liquidation and neutralisation of any illusions of transcendence (and thus, of religion, especially Christendom: that is, salvation from above). However, in that precise sense, it is possible to say that Nietzsche and Marx carry the very Hegelian project of modernity to its final consequences (that is, the project of immanence), and thereby reach a conclusion precisely opposed to Hegel's theodicy; while, on the other hand, Schelling's and Kierkegaard's kenotic eschatologies attempt at the impossible restitution of a Christianity, at the epochal closure of modernity, which will always remain decisively a polemical event against the immanentising project of modernity. Karl Löwith brings out the proximity and distance between Marx's eschatology without God and Kierkegaard's Christian eschatology in the following manner:

> To the bankruptcy of this 'world grown old', Marx opposed the proletariat; Kierkegaard, solitary existence before God . . . reduction of human existence to the elementary questions, to the bare question of existence as such; this was for Kierkegaard the other side of what Marx called the 'secular question as to the value of life'. Thus both criticisms are based on the same hostility toward the existing order; to Marx's secular criticism of the bourgeois-capitalist world there corresponds Kierkegaard's equally radical criticism of the bourgeois-Christian world, which is as far removed from primitive Christianity as the bourgeois state is from the *polis*. Marx confronts the external, existential situation of the masses with a decision, and Kierkegaard the internal, existential relationship of the individual to himself; Marx philosophizes without God and Kierkegaard before God. (Löwith 1991: 160–1)

One can, thus, say that Kierkegaardian 'polemics against Hegel's process' is something like

> an anticommunist manifesto. He went so far as to predict the danger which would come when the catastrophe broke ; false prophets of Christianity will then arise, inventors of a new religion, who, infected with demons, will arrogantly declare themselves apostles, like thieves in the costume of police. Thanks to their promises, they will receive terrible support from the age, until it finally becomes clear that the age stands in need of the absolute, and of a truth which is equally valid for all ages. With this view toward a restoration of Christendom through martyr-witnesses who allow themselves to be slain for the truth, Kierkegaard is the contemporary antithesis to Marx's propaganda of a proletarian world revolution. As the actual strength of Communism, Kierkegaard saw the 'ingredient' of Christian religiosity which it still contained. (Ibid.: 114)

'In these times everything is political': this sentence of Kierkegaard (quoted by Taubes 2009: 173) sounds like Marx's. 'Only religion is different from politics, as different as heaven is from earth, by virtue of its starting point and its final goal. For politics begins on earth in order to remain on earth, while religion "deduces its origin from above, and transfiguring the earthly, seeks to raise it up to heaven"' (Taubes 2009: 173).

This is why the Nietzschean and Marxist 'atheistic' eschatologies often appear to be more 'radical', for they appear to think outside Christianity altogether and, therefore, outside of any theological foundation of political hegemonies. On the other hand, the Schellingian and Kierkegaardian political theologies, which eschatologically put into question any political *auctoritus* (for both Schelling and Kierkegaard the state as well as the visible Church – insofar as the latter allies itself with the former – belong to the same profane order at the level of world-historical politics) on the theological foundation, in the name of an event that never, rigorously thought, belongs to history (because it marks the birth of history itself), their eschatologies have a 'radicality' that will always exceed any immanentising and secularising project of any epoch; in other words, they can be said to have the 'radicality' to put into question any political sovereignty of any world-historical epoch.

This shows, in clearer light now, the decisive importance of the event of 'exit' – and the other 'inauguration' outside metaphysics – carried out by Schelling: while one line from Schellingian eschatology goes to the 'atheistic' Marxist eschatology (Frank 1975), whether it is Marx himself or 'the Marxist Schelling' (Habermas 1985: 61–78) Ernst Bloch (2000, 2009); the other line, carried over by Kierkegaard and by Franz Rosenzweig, develops religious 'deconstruction' (kenotic Christology of Kierkegaard, and messianism of Rosenzweig) of any political theology of sovereignty. This truly shows the Proteus character of Schellingian thought. In that sense, even the Nietzschean – and Marx's – atheistic 'exit' from metaphysics that accompanies his deconstruction of (Hegelian) theodicy can be said to be indebted to the *kenosis* and the caesura that Schelling introduces between 'the negative' and 'the positive' philosophy, and that opens, in still another manner, the abyss of the unconscious (McGrath 2012).

Therefore, to understand not only the development of Kierkegaard's political eschatology of *kenosis* but the very development of the post-Hegelian thinking which is concerned with 'the exit' of philosophy, it is necessary to appreciate fully the political eschatology of Schellingian 'actuality without potentiality'. What, then, are the essential elements of Schelling's political eschatology?

The political theology of Schelling

To understand the political eschatology of Schelling, it is helpful to begin with the fundamental proposition of his eschatology: that the dominant tendency of the Occidental metaphysics determines being as potentiality. The epoch of modernity – modernity that has secularised the theological concepts in terms of immanent theodicy of history – understands and determines potentiality (which is not 'a' potentiality among other potentialities of being but the very potentiality of being at all) as Subject. This epoch of modernity, and along with it the Occidental metaphysics as such, has now come to a closure, both in the sense of having fulfilled itself and having terminated itself thereby, opening to a sense of pure exteriority or pure transcendence. It is in Schelling, in a way for the first time and in its own way, in a singular and irreducible way, such closure comes to make itself manifest; in other words, it comes to certain *phenomenality*. This *phenomenalisation* takes place precisely at the instance – where the instance itself is an abyss, a *wink*, an eschatological opening to eternity – when the 'idea' of 'actuality without potentiality' presents itself in Schellingian works, an idea that interrupts and momentarily arrests the univocity of the discourse of metaphysics. This means nothing other than the following: the *phenomenalisation* at the closure of metaphysics, or the *phenomenalisation* of the closure of metaphysics, is, at the same time, the apparition of a caesura, or a hiatus between what Schelling comes to name towards the end of his life as 'positive philosophy' and 'negative philosophy'. This caesura cuts through the immanence of the discourse of modernity by an un-pre-thinkable (*Unvordenkliche*) de-cision (*Ent-Scheidung*): the result is a 'political theology' of an eschatological delegitimation of any earthly sovereign power on the basis of theological foundation.

The Schellingian 'deconstructive phenomenology' or 'phenomenological deconstruction' – the task of which is that of making manifest the epochal closure of the constituted phenomenality (a paradoxical phenomenology it is, for it makes manifest that which is foreclosed in the constituted order of phenomenality) – can be said to have a twofold task:

1. On the one hand, to decisively put into question the fundamental metaphysical principle of Hegelian theodicy of history, namely, the immanence of potentiality, for it is in Hegelian theodicy of history, so contends Schelling, the Occidental metaphysics comes to realise itself in its utmost possibility. This demands rethinking of potentiality, or radicalising potentiality, without abandoning it, and, yet, without making potentiality 'the sovereign referent' or the 'hegemonic fantasm'

(Schürmann 2003) of the epoch of modernity: without having to make potentiality the legitimising *arché* of the epoch of modernity.
2. This demands, at the same time, in a mode of reversal to the former, and yet, transcending the gesture of mere reversal at the same time, that we think 'actuality without potentiality', actuality in which there is no potentiality: a radical transcendence, infinity itself, an exception – like the Platonic 'Good beyond being' – that does not become in turn rule. This exception, which does not serve as the legitimating principle of hegemonies, nor of the order of constituted phenomenality in turn, can't be understood as 'onto' and 'theological' ground of beings, whether as 'nature', or as 'reason' or as 'Subject': an exceptional and un-pre-thinkable (*Unvordenkliche*) exuberance of 'beyond' or 'over-being' (*Überseyn*). If this is so, then the 'beyond' or 'over-being' can't be an ontological principle; it can't even be thought of as 'principle': the actuality exposes all the potentialities of being – and the very potentiality of being, and the being of potentiality – to the groundlessness of inscrutable, sublime freedom.

This double task, to be carried out at the same instance, comes to introduce, in the wake of Schelling, the decisive caesura into the fundamental ground of the Occidental metaphysics; that is: the caesura into the univocity of Being. This has led Schelling – foreshadowing Marx, Nietzsche, Heidegger and also Kierkegaard – to make the 'gesture' of (what we can call, borrowing the word from Marx) the 'exit' (*Ausgang*) from/of philosophy (Bensussan 2007): philosophy (as 'system' or as 'ontology') can't think actuality *as* actuality; that is, 'actuality without potentiality' (which is neither mere potential actuality nor mere representation of actuality).

The double gestures of Schellingian 'deconstruction', complex as they are, while radically putting into question the immanence of Hegelian theodicy of history thinks of an exception which is, nevertheless, without sovereignty: the 'actuality without potentiality' that Schelling thinks of is neither the actuality of the concrete political order that Schmitt speaks of (this is what distinguishes Schmitt from his interlocutor Hans Blumenberg who is the thinker of metaphor) nor is it tied to the 'nomos of the earth'; it does not have any analogy with any order of potentiality. Like the Pauline idea of *kenosis*, the exceptional actuality of *Überseyn* in all its exuberance empties out all the attributes of potentiality that fascinate our gaze with its 'hegemonic fantasm'. It opens up, by radically suspending the order of worldly *nomos*, to 'the singularization to come' (Schürmann 2003) where the hegemonic principle withers away, uncoupled from the law of *Koinon*. This mode of thinking, which comes to Schelling via Meister Eckhart, consists of a distinction made between God as the principle or *arché* of beings (as *hegemonikon*: the sovereign principle, or the principle of sovereignty that founds the order of creation) and, on the other hand, the idea of a Godhead without sovereignty (without principle and without *arché*). We must learn to exist without principle and without *arché*: 'The rose does have no why; it blossoms without reason/Forgetful of itself, oblivious to our vision' (Angelus Silesius 1986: 54).

Between the Godhead (whose exuberance – un-pre-thinkable – is beyond being) and God (the nature of God, or the God of nature, God as the governing principle of the world) there is neither analogy nor any (Neo-Platonic) emanation but an irreducible abyss: the theologico-political principle of *analogia entis* can't explain the abyss of the difference in God himself, not to speak of any possible analogia at all between the exception of the divine and any earthly sovereignty. Only by rigorous mortification of our will and all forms of egotism is it possible to participate, by a gratuitous grace, in the *beatitude to come* which is, for Schelling, the eschatological event par excellence (Schelling 2010). The essence of religion, and the fundamental vocation for philosophy, in two different ways, lies in this infinite task of mortification of any earthly claims to sovereignty. The crucial word here is 'abandonment' (*Gelassenheit*) that even Heidegger, following Eckhart and Schelling, makes the decisive word for his later thinking: we must abandon not only the world, and empty out all the worldly attributes but even God (God insofar as he is mere nature, and as the mere ground of beings, God as no more than the nomothetic and monothetic ground of the worldly existence): the glory of the Lord is *kenosis*! This infinite paradox – which is the paralysis of worldly potentialities and vertigo of thought – is the very essence of religion, and also of philosophy; in two different ways they are oriented towards the event *to come*; namely, the infinite and gratuitous gift of beatitude. What arrives, as an eschatological event and as pure generosity, infinitely exceeds not only the totality of beings but 'being' itself. Hence, there is not only no possible *analogia entis* between the two 'orders', the Godhead is not even 'entis' at all: the 'onto-theological constitution of metaphysics' has come here to a decisive failure.

Eschatology, then, is the heart of religion. Understanding religion eschatologically thus, Schelling carefully distinguishes it – as early as his lectures on the philosophy of art of 1804 – from myth: religion, or better, the eschatological event *to come*, interrupts the mythic-political foundation of the worldly order, and empties out, *kenotically*, any sovereign claims of worldly potentialities. This subtraction (emptying out) is also an infinite excess – over potentiality as such, which, unlike the worldly order of the mythic-political, is not an auto-constitutional origin of the *nomos* but is Love: Love does not rule over life by violently imprisoning us in the cages of necessity but places us in radical freedom. The theologico-political apparatus of the worldly order, mythically founded, is eschatologically burst open, and is rendered non-autochthonous and non-sovereign, and is exposed open to the *that* which *ex-sists*, ecstatically, without *potestas*: namely, to the 'actuality without potentiality', to the exception which is without sovereignty.

As early as 1804 Schelling decisively puts into question the theologico-political consequences that arise from the Neo-Platonic idea of emanation as the generative principle of the world. Plotinus explicates the generation of the phenomenal order and its relation to its origin as the continuous diminishing of the absolute light. But, this way of understanding the eternal birth of the phenomenal order and its relation to the absolute does not serve to explain satisfactorily the very possibility of radical evil, because:

> In the absolute world there are no confines anywhere and just as God can only bring forth the real-per-se and absolute, so any ensuing effulgence is again absolute and can itself only bring forth something akin to it. There can be no continuous passage into the exact opposite, the absolute privation of all reality, nor can the finite arise from the infinite by decrements. (Schelling 2010: 24)

Only the idea of an irreducible *distance* or *remove* (*Abfall*) – which also means apostasy or falling away) – can serve as the explicative principle of not only the coming into being of the phenomenal order but also the very possibility (and actuality) of radical evil. Gnostic-Kabbalistic in inspiration, which is farther intensified through his reading of Jacob Böhme (Scholem 1995: 412), the idea of *falling away* makes impossible any attempt to embody the divine on the immanent plane of world-historical politics, for it undoes in advance any possible analogy between the absolute and the phenomenal order: not only the Hegelian immanent theodicy of history but also the Schmittean political theology of transcendence receive here a decisive un-doing.

Schelling elaborates this antinomic idea in much more detail in his 1810 private lectures in Stuttgart. The emergence of the world is not explained by the generative principle of continuity but by a divine un-pre-thinkable de-cision: by a fundamental *(de)cision* or *separation* the world comes into being that *sets apart* being (*das Seyende*) from Being (*Seyn*). The emergence of the world is *set apart* from the groundless foundation: such must be the divine freedom which, by a *constriction* or *withdrawal* of itself – more out of his abyss of Love than out of divine *potestas* – lets the world come into being! That is to say: divine aban*don*ment of sovereign power, and abounding Love, given in pure *donation*, is the origin of the phenomenal order. The coming into being of the world which, in a sense, is 'non-divine' (though without God there is no 'is') – where any 'is' is also, in a sense, non-being – lies less in the overwhelming and majestic divine power than in an un-pre-thinkable (*Unvordenkliche*) renunciation of divine force so that the creaturely being 'be': the divine empties itself and subtracts its own sovereignty, so that the phenomenal order, which in a way outside divinity, may come into being at all. In other words: God(head) im-potentiates himself and reduces himself to non-sovereignty – by rendering himself weak – so that something outside himself may 'be', and that 'something' – whose being is, in a way, 'non-being' – 'is' such that its very being is 'loaned'; as such, no being in the worldly order can claim for itself autochthony and an aboriginal existence. As 'loaned' being (whose very being is 'loaned', and to that extent is 'non-being'), any being in the worldly order – even the earthly sovereign figure – is that whose possibility is never actualisable: hence is the infinite veil of melancholy of all earthly creatures (Schelling 1936: 79). Actuality where there no potentiality is left, does not belong as 'capacity' or 'possession' to any worldly being: it is the consummate fire where any sovereign claim of the worldly power is burnt and annihilated, not by the violence of divine *potestas*, but by the divine violence of Love which, while annihilating, also redeems it. At work here is not only the Heraclitean fire but also the Pauline opposition between the spirit and the letter, and *pistis* and *nomos*.

The event of the Fall marks – so Schelling continues in his 1810 private lectures – the breakage or fissure into the nexus of beings (God-man-nature): the jointure of beings is disjoined. This disjointure is the origin of the historical order, the unredeemed state of destitution and evil which has its analogy, in the realm of nature, its sickness: what sickness in the realm of nature is, evil is in the order of history. As Stanislas Breton rightly points out, Schellingian phenomenology of nature here is Pauline in inspiration: nature as the order of 'passing away' and in fallen and unredeemed state is groaning and crying for redemption (Breton 2011: 124). As the order that can't ground itself on its immanent foundation, the apostate state of history is the realm of mere 'passing away' and transiency: it is what must, anyway, by the very logic of its origin, pass away, and is passing away; no 'figure' in the apostate order of world-historical existence can claim sovereignty without, ultimately, having to pass away. It is here we see Schellingian theologico-political deduction of the state and the Church.

The state is the mortal being's impoverished attempt to supplement an absolute impoverishment; namely, the link or the jointure that is broken among beings as consequence of the Fall. As such, the state is, like anything in the profane order, transient: it is this supplement that forcefully tries to affect the lost unity by always making 'legitimate' use of power, which is the source of violence. Far from seeing the state as the figure of the absolute, the state is thought here as precarious and fragile (the order of non-being), and precisely thereby it is being dangerous and tyrannical: the evil of the state lies not in the power of its being, but in its malicious, devouring hunger for being. This totalising tendency is the intrinsic logic of its very '(non)being'; the state is necessarily and potentially – because it is ruled by power alone – unjust and tyrannical: that means that any worldly regime, ruled by any earthly sovereign power, is always potentially wrong.

What the state is in the external realm, the Church is in the internal realm: an attempt to supplement the lost nexus among beings. The insufficient and precarious character of the state which is instituted as a supplement of the lost nexus of beings demands the second revelation to restore the lost unity: here Christ being the mediator between God and man, himself God-man, dying the most ignoble death on the cross, and bearing the intolerable suffering and evil only to redeem the unredeemed condition of the fallen state. So, the Church is the immediate consequence of the second revelation. But insofar as the Church, in the process of its historical evolution as institution, takes part in negotiations with worldly *potestas* and allies itself with the state, it forgets its initial eschatological impulse – that burning desire for the end of the unjust world, and for the freedom from the earthly ties (both ties with the sovereign power of the Roman Empire, and the family ties of *oikonomia*) – and becomes just like any other worldly institution: the Church here becomes the very theological foundation of worldly sovereignties. Schellingian deconstruction of the theologico-political legitimation of worldly sovereignty is nowhere as explicit as here. Far from deifying the profane order of the world-historical becoming, and far from seeing the modern state of Prussia as the embodiment of divine reason, Schelling here argues – contra Hegel – for separation of the theological from the political realm. This separation alone can redress the 'political tyranny' and the horror of universal domination:

> In surveying more recent history, which with good reason, is said to begin with the arrival of Christianity in Europe, we note that humanity had to pass through two stages in its attempt to discover or produce a unity; first that of producing an internal unity through the Church, which had to fail because the Church simultaneously sought to become the external unity and eventually attempted to produce external unity by means of the state. Only with the demise of hierarchical [systems] has the state attained this importance, and it is manifest that the pressure of political tyranny has increased ever since in exact proportion to the belief that an inner unity seemed dispensable; indeed it is bound to increase to a maximum intensity until, perhaps, upon the collapse of these one-dimensional attempts humanity will discover the right way. (Schelling 1994: 229)

And therefore,

> God, however, as identity of the highest order, remains above all reality and eternally has merely an indirect relationship. If then in the higher moral order the State represents a *second nature*, then the divine can never have anything other than an indirect relationship to it; never can it bear any real relationship to it, and religion, if it seeks to preserve itself in unscathed pure ideality, can therefore never exist – even in the most perfect State – other than esoterically in the form of *mystery cults*. (Schelling 2010: 51)

Here lies the essence of Schellingian 'negative political theology': religion, eschatologically understood, is the promised religion – the *religion to come* – which refuses to be embodied in any given order of worldly hegemonies:

> Whatever the ultimate goal may turn out to be, this much is certain, namely, that true unity can be attained only *via* the path of religion; only the supreme and most diverse culture of religious knowledge will enable humanity, if not to abolish the state outright, then at least to ensure that the state will progressively divest itself of the blind force that governs it, and to transfigure this force into intelligence. It is not that the Church ought to dominate the state or vice-versa, but that the state ought to cultivate the religious principles within itself and that the community of all peoples ought to be founded on religious convictions that, themselves, ought to become universal. (Schelling 1994: 229)

The caesura that Schelling explicitly introduces between 'the negative' and 'the positive philosophy' in his Berlin lectures (1841–54) – though the germ of this distinction can be traced back to his incomplete magnum opus *Die Weltalter* – is based upon the distinction that he makes between *quid sit* (what a being is) and *quod sit* (that it is): while *quid sit*, in its infinite potentiality or capacity to be, can be grasped (*greifen*) by the power of the concept (*Begriff* – which means grasping or seizing: the concept seizes and grasps), *quod sit* refuses the potentiality of the concept's self-grasping. Here is Schelling's decisive confrontation with Hegelian onto-theological foundation of metaphysics. The Hegelian concept of the concept – the Absolute Concept, the Absolute Concept as infinite negativity (where the negation arrives at the absolute by a dialectical self-cancellation) – can grasp, in its auto-grasping, only the *dunamis* (that is, the immanent auto-movement) of being-in-its infinite potentiality-to-be: the metaphysical violence of the (Hegelian) concept (grasping, seizing, appropriating) can measure up to being only insofar as being is being-in-its-power (being as potentiality), that is, the whatness (*quid sit*) of being; the concept determines – by negating the negation, in an immanent movement of self-cancellation of the negative – only the essence, the whatness, of being. But the immeasurable actuality of being, the *that* (*Daß*), in all its exuberance, refuses the measure of the concept, for it doesn't need any potentiality to be: 'the former – the answer to the question of *what* it is – accords me into the *essence* of the thing, or it provides that I understand the thing, that I have an understanding or a concept of it, or have it *itself* within the concept. The other insight however, *that* it is, does not accord me just the concept but rather something that goes beyond just the concept, which is existence' (Schelling 2007: 129). This actuality of existence which is neither the *telos* of an immanent movement of the negative nor the conditioned-hypothetic ('if being were to exist . . .') being 'is', rigorously speaking, not even 'being' but 'beyond-being'(*Überseyn*): a pure and unconditional generosity *that* ex-sists prior to any potentiality (to-be), and that groundlessly keeps the very order of being open to transcendence! This transcendence of actuality can't be determined to have resulted from the immanent movement of auto-generative negation (this was Hegel's confusion, who thought in an inverted manner), for one can't conceive the radical positive as arising out of the self-cancellation of the negation. What Hegel's *Logic* can achieve, at the end of the auto-generative movement of the negation, is only the conceptual-logical actuality, which is still only 'conceptual', while the radical actuality without potentiality is still outside of the *telos*, because it is *always already* (that is, immemorially), at the very beginning of the movement, excluded from the immanence of potentiality: this is why Schelling calls it 'exuberance' and 'un-pre-thinkable' (*Unvordenkliche*). What Hegel's system can achieve at best – given that even concept can have movement, but only a conceptual movement (while Hegel thought that it is actual-real movement) – is what results from the self-cancellation of 'not-not': that is, what is still a 'not-not', though at a higher degree of making explicit what is an immanent potentiality; if it is positive, it is still a potentially positive, which Aristotle grasped much more profoundly than Hegel. Thus, he (Aristotle) renounced the *Daß* from the purest fire of his rigorous analysis (without pretending to have grasped it). What returns in the Hegelian self-cancelling movement of 'not not' is the circular return of potentialities, while the exuberant excess of the immeasurable actuality disrupts, or interrupts, this circular return of potentiality, and exposes it open to what exceeds its closure: to the actuality without potentiality. The mythic violence of potentiality that returns, in ever new mode, to the same, is radically interrupted and is burst open, apocalyptically, to its radical outside. The horror of the eternal return of the same in its vicious circling and re-circling can only be redeemed by an arrival of that which is absolutely heterogeneous, which does not need any potentiality-to-exist: it must radically suspend the mythic foundation of potentiality that constitutes the law.

As Heidegger rightly remarked, Schelling has remained and will remain the unique and singular thinker of the West. If the *arché* of Reason constitutes the hegemonic fantasm of the epochal condition of modernity, then by opening the principle of Reason to that which ex-sists, ecstatically, without a 'why', Schelling makes destitute the hegemony of modernity: 'actuality without potentiality' can't be grasped, unlike the essences of entities, by the principle of Reason. And we have seen how Schelling, conversely, equally makes destitute the theologico-political exception of legitimacy that threatens to become the rule. Irreducible to worldly potentialities, the sovereignty of divine actuality is at once a *kenosis*, that is, non-sovereign: without this, even the emergence of the phenomenal order can't be explicated. Only by abandonment – of all worldly *potestas* – and by rigorous mortification of the will can a mortal participate in beatitude, which is the highest vocation and the highest gift for the mortals. This mortification is the fire that does not annihilate us, but redeems us through its work of purification, and releases us from the cages of the world. The fire of exuberance 'beyond being' is the Good which precedes even the distinction between good and evil: already in an 1807 essay on human freedom Schelling elaborates this fundamental and unique thought of his. To participate in the highest gift possible for the mortal – which, as a gift, exceeds any economy of the worldly order – it is necessary that all the worldly attributes must enter destitution. As Eckhart says – and as does Schelling in the following – one must abandon even God:

> He who wishes to place himself in the beginning of a truly free philosophy must abandon even God. Here we say: who wishes to maintain it, he will lose it; and who gives up, he will find it. Only he has come to the ground of himself and has known the whole depth of life who has once abandoned everything, and has himself been abandoned by everything. He for whom everything disappeared and who saw himself alone with the infinite: a great step which Plato compared to death. (Quoted by Heidegger 1985: 6–7)

From Hegel to Kierkegaard

To understand the caesura which Kierkegaard himself introduces – and which we will discuss in much more detail a little later – it is important to understand the caesura that Schelling unleashes at the very heart of 'philosophy' between 'the positive' and 'the negative'. And we have seen above the immense theologico-political consequences that arise from this irreducible caesura between that event of actuality without potentiality and that mythic circle of potentiality that returns to the same. By interrupting eschatologically the horror of the circular return of potentiality to the same, the event of actuality releases human existence from the cages of the mythic violence of the law and places it in freedom which is gifted to the human as a 'loan' (Schelling 1936). The caesuras that Schelling and Kierkegaard introduce, each in his own manner and according to his own fashion, are inspired by Lutheran *destructio* which we know to be Pauline in spirit (of Galatians and of Romans): it is this Pauline *destructio* that haunts the univocity of being (which is the very task of metaphysics) and reintroduces, at the epochal closure of modernity, the 'separation' and 'setting apart' that explodes the Hegelian immanence of self-presence. The irreducible non-contemporaneous and non-identical event disrupts vertically – cuts through – the immanent universe of the Absolute Concept. The explosive character of the event (Kierkegaard calls it 'incendiary' or 'conflagration'), ungraspable in the economy of knowledge and excess to any calculable-programmable *telos* of world-historical theodicy of history, has something eschatological about it, but no longer in the same terms that modernity gives to it. It rather attempts to rethink, in an impossible manner, the event as *stasis*: not as an intra-mundane world-historical event grasped in the Absolute Concept, but as the eschatological judgement upon history that explodes the immanent foundation of the world and delivers it to divine freedom. Both Schelling and Kierkegaard, each in his own manner, call this explosive event – which can't be a logical category of an ontological system, and which does not participate in the dialectical movement of mediation between the particular and the universal – 'actuality' (*Wirklichkeit*): it is the event of freedom in which our exposure (that tears us away from our satisfaction in the Absolute Concept, or in world-historical politics of infinite progress) to the arrival of the Other *surprises* us; it is this event of non-analogy (which has no worldly incarnation, which does not figure in any worldly figures) that Luther, in a Pauline spirit, makes the worldly order and the worldly truth of triumph inglorious, while the true glory is thought to be the paradoxical *kenosis* which empties out all potentiality of the law mythically founded. What, then, comes to make itself manifest – where manifestation itself retains an irreducible characteristic of '*absconditus*' or 'incognito' (hence it is the paradox of infinity!) – is *that* which is denied in the mythic order of 'constituted phenomenality': the tragic singularity itself – of the exceptional event of divine decision which consists of the total abandonment on the cross – which, eschatologically, remains non-contemporaneously contemporary to each epoch: it is irreducibly distant, a distance immeasurable and abyssal, from each world-historical epoch, and yet, precisely for that matter, it also thereby keeps the promise of fulfilment (*pleroma*) in the end an imminent possibility (*eschaton*). By not-identifying itself with the *telos* of the world-historical politics of progress, this event of the end retains its paradox of being at once an infinite distance and an infinite proximity which affirms an affirmation that, nevertheless, does not assume a positive statement (against a negative statement).

It is now understandable why Schelling's use of the word 'actuality' in his second lecture on revelation made the heart of Kierkegaard leap up in joy. Both Schelling and Kierkegaard name that finite being who is torn open by divine freedom from the order of 'constituted phenomenality' (from the mythic order of the law) as 'existence': the event of being that is absolved from the world-order of totality and from the conceptual order of universality (for Kierkegaard, that event of being which is released from the aesthetic enjoyment in the worldly beauty and from the consolation for the loss of its immediacy in the ethical universality: hence is the necessity of the third stage!). For both Schelling and Kierkegaard, the singular event of existence is not a conceptual category; it does not become a category in the immanent movement of potentialities. The event is neither an ontological process nor a logical movement: actuality is neither movement nor process. While Hegel grasped the event(s) on the basis of 'onto-theological' movement or process, both Schelling and Kierkegaard think of movement on the basis of the event – of actuality. The event as actuality is, thus, de-formalised and non-totalised. Arising out of the abyss of freedom, itself-free, the event is Spirit. Hegel too describes the very phenomenological movement itself as the 'phenomenology of spirit', but between the Schellingian-Kierkegaardian idea of the Spirit and the Hegelian Spirit there is a qualitative distinction. This distinction is also a theologico-political de-cision. In it lies Kierkegaard's – more prominently than in Schelling – opposition to the epoch of modernity, his opposition to the secularised legitimacy of political powers on a (Christian) theological foundation.

This intensification of eschatological difference – difference that renders impossible any continuous-immanent passage of passing – is Kierkegaard's (who follows Schelling here rather closely) decisively polemical response to the Hegelian speculative-dialectical principle of 'reconciliation'. While Hegel could achieve the reconciliation of the dialectical opposites – subjective and objective, inner and outer, infinite and finite – on the theological foundation ('speculative Good Friday'), the harmony achieved here is only the conceptual harmony of the opposed concepts; as mere conceptual harmony, it leaves behind the explosive sting of *actuality* which always remains, in regard to the concept, an indigestible remainder, an inhospitable remnant. In the objective order of the political realm there is nothing to prevent this conceptual harmony – which is, as we have seen, achieved through theological means – from serving as the apology of the world as it exists; or, it even can be used to justify, at least on a metaphysical foundation, the order of constituted phenomenality as it exists. The harmony of the political realm, based upon this ontological abuse of certain theological principle, can be achieved only at an immense price: that of leaving behind the inhospitable remainder of actuality, the irreducible remnant of the event of existence, and that of reducing religion to a political means. In such harmony God is made to become either the legislative principle of the world, or a regulative principle of the world, but as *arché* (*principium*) nevertheless it remains (the principle on which every hegemony is founded): one can still trace back the worldly attributes of our historical-political being to an ultimate hegemonic fantasm that keeps the world-order harmonious, well-rounded and aesthetically justifying. It is this fantastication of God – or religion – that Schelling and Kierkegaard effectively put into question. In Hegel's theodicy of history, God becomes a fantasm, and when Hegel sees in the modern state of Prussia a figure of the Absolute, he – the official professor of philosopher – only sees a fantasm; he sees a fantastic harmony in the world-order where there is none: he forgets the original offensive passion of Christianity as scandal on the cross, as revolt against the world as it exists, and its non-dialectical martyrdom against the sovereign figures of the world-historical politics.

Following Schelling, the harmony of the world-order as the order of constituted phenomenality, at least achieved at the level of the Concept in Hegel's system, falls to pieces in Marx's communist and Kierkegaard's anticommunist manifesto: while for Marx the 'outside' of the system is in the world, for Kierkegaard the 'outside' of the system is the 'outside' of the world. Therefore, Kierkegaard could say – as if confronting Marx here – that radical equality, which is the qualitative event par excellence, can never be achieved in the world by mere human-political means through a proletarian revolution, for as the qualitative event, radical equality is never an intra-mundane affair. In these two different – even opposed – ways it is always the question of the 'outside' here: that is, of an exteriority of actuality which is not an attenuated variation of potentiality, actuality which cannot be thought to be a result (*telos*) of potentiality and is, thus, not a potential actuality. It is this *actuality without potentiality* which is introduced by the later Schelling where it is the question of taking an 'exit' from the ontological monism, an exit which opens it to the infinity exteriority outside totality. The exteriority – which for Kierkegaard, and for Schelling, does not become a worldly figure in the profane order – puts into question the injustice of the anonymous order of constituted phenomenality, and eschatologically brings the violence of the world-order under the judgement. The harmonious world-order, even though it is achieved only at a conceptual level by Hegel, is here shattered. The result is the thought of exception – and decision – which is without sovereignty: a negative political theology.

Note

1. Thus Nietzsche writes in 'On the Uses and Disadvantages of History for Life': 'The belief that one is a latecomer of the ages is, in any case, paralyzing and depressing but it must appear dreadful and devastating when such a belief one day by a bold inversion raises this latecomer to a Godhead as the true meaning and goal of all previous events, when his miserable condition is equated with a completion of world-history. Such a point of view has accustomed the Germans to talk of a "world process" and to justify their own age as the necessary result of this world-process; such a point of view has set history, insofar as history is "the concept that realizes itself", "the dialectics of the spirit of the peoples", and the "world-tribunal", in place of the other spiritual powers, art and religion, as the sole sovereign power. History understood in this Hegelian fashion has been mockingly called God's sojourn on earth, though the god referred to has been created only by history. This god, however, became transparent and comprehensible to himself within the Hegelian craniums and has already ascended all the dialectically possible steps of his evolution up to this self-revelation: so that for Hegel the climax and terminus of the world-process coincided with his own existence in Berlin. Indeed, he ought to have said that everything that came after him was properly to be considered merely as a musical coda to the world-historical rondo or, even more properly, as superfluous. He did not say it: instead he implanted into the generation thoroughly leavened by him that admiration for the "power of history" which in practice transforms every moment into a naked admiration for success and leads to an idolatry of the factual: which idolatry is now generally described by the very mythological yet quite idiomatic expression "to accommodate oneself to the facts". But he who has learned to bend his back and bow his head before the "power of history" at last nods "Yes" like Chinese mechanical doll to every power, whether it be a government or public opinion or a numerical majority, and moves his limbs to the precise rhythm at which any "power" whatever pulls the strings. If every success is a rational necessity, if every event is a victory of the logical or the "idea" – then down on your knees quickly and do reverence to the whole stepladder of "success"!' (Nietzsche 1997: 104–5).

Chapter 2

Event and Existence

The violence of the concept

In his *Negative Dialectics* (1981) Theodor Adorno brings out the innermost connection between the logical operation of the concept and the operation of the law: that of the logic of subsumption which subsumes the heterogeneous multiplicity of phenomena under the unitary concept, denuding the non-identical sensuousness of the singular phenomenon and its eventive eruption in and from the midst of the world. The concept is, then, the metaphysical paradigm of the law; its violence consists in its denial of the event of phenomenality, which always is singular, under the regime of constituted phenomenality. The event, arising *in* the midst of the world, is, then, not *of* the world: it sets the world *apart* from itself, from its given ground, and renders the world non-co-incident with what now exceeds it. The violence of the *separation* with which the event flares up – the incendiary fire that separates the unity of the ground – is qualitatively different from the violence of the law. This is why Schelling makes a distinction between fire and fire: the former annihilates without atonement, and the latter atones and consummates without annihilation; or, as between the two kinds of violence that Walter Benjamin speaks of: there is a violence that is 'bloody, the latter is lethal without spilling blood' (Benjamin 1986: 297); the former the mythic violence of the law, and the latter the messianic-divine violence of exception without sovereignty. The denial of the other – the singular, that which exceeds the blood-life of the existent, the heterogeneous and the irreducible outside the law – gives rise to what Reiner Schürmann calls 'hegemony', the order of constituted phenomenality, where singulars are dialectically reduced to the particular instantiations of the universal. Dialectic that works through 'mediation' and 'reconciliation', between the universal and the particular, is the enemy of the event: it violently denies the future eruption (or, the eruption of the future) by pre-giving all phenomena a necessary law of movement. Schelling calls this necessary movement of concepts/categories that immanently reach out towards closure the movement of potentiality, which is the task of 'negative philosophy' (Hegel is the master thinker of potentiality); while the other, the event of singularity that absolves itself from the order of totality of potencies, and that refuses, in an un-pre-thinkable manner, to be enclosed within the order of constituted phenomenality, is called by him 'actuality without potentiality': the latter, in its exuberance and ecstasy, remains un-enclosed in the force of the law, in the violence of the gaze that emanates from the power of the *hegemonikon*. Anticipating Kierkegaard as much as Heidegger, Rosenzweig as much as the early Bloch, Schelling comes to call this exuberant event of phenomenality 'existence': existence not merely opposed to essence nor as its mere inversion; the essence of existence is rather the eventive phenomenality that absolves itself from the order of totality and, as such, is infinity itself. Existence, out of its finitude, is exposed open to the infinity; it traverses through the passage of finitude, suffers through it as the necessary mortification of those categories, attributes or predicates that the *hegemonikon* imposes upon life: as if, as it were, these categories, attributes or predicates have to enter mortification or destitution (*kenosis*) that burst open the cages of the law. What exceeds this violence of the constituted phenomenality and, thus, what exceeds the metaphysical violence of the concept (*Begriff*) that grasps phenomena as mere particulars belonging to the universal, is *justice* or *love*. Justice and love, in twofold manners, are the exceptions in regard to the constituted order of the law: they un-grasp existence from the grasp (*greifen*) of the concept and release it from its violence of subsumption. The essence of existence is this un-grasping or de-linking, *separation* and *setting apart* (in the sense of what Kierkegaard calls 'inter-esse'); it passes through this passage of death, which is not mere conceptual power of death that Hegel speaks of as the work of negativity that converts even nothingness into being, but the passage that makes the actual an *actuality*; it is the *actuality* of the actual, as Schelling would have said in his Berlin lectures, and which Kierkegaard heard when his heart leapt up in joy. Existence is, each time, its very actuality. This actuality consists of not a necessary movement on the scale of immanence, but an infinite transcendence of all *theologoumenon* (which wants to exhaust the divine in the infinite proliferation of divine names). In that sense, this infinity of transcendence is abandonment of categories, attributes or predicates that want to name the name: it is, as such, *abandonment* par excellence. Existence is trained in and through mortification, through various stages of life, as Kierkegaard would say. The various stages of life are not successive but simultaneous (such is the event):[1] they are various stages of *askesis* through which we abandon the phantasms that constitute the order of *hegemonikon*. Abandonment abandons the sovereign phantasm of the law which grounds the hegemonic order of constituted phenomenality. Therefore, it is necessary to think existence at the closure of metaphysics: *the event of existence* – for existence is to be understood in the infinity of its verbal resonance rather than as entities grasped in categories (what Martin Heidegger names in *Sein und Zeit* as *Vorhandenheit*) – is also the event of releasement: out of the abyss of freedom, existence is each time a true learning to abandon each 'why' of the hegemonic phantasm. Abandonment releases the event of phenomenality from the violence of the concept, thereby abandoning metaphysics to itself.

The *spacing* of existence

> There can be no system for life itself ... existence is the *spacing* that holds things apart; the systematic is the finality that joins them together. (Kierkegaard 2009b: 100; italics mine)

With the question of existence, where existence itself is the question of thinking as much of existing itself par excellence, Kierkegaard not merely inverts the metaphysical privilege given to essence (thereby having to operate within the history of metaphysics), but rather releases existence from the law of the concept that grounds the hegemonic regime of metaphysics: in this sense, the indebtedness of Kierkegaard to later Schellingian thinking goes beyond his explicit acknowledgement. Existence must be thought beyond and outside the enclosed circle of mobile concepts (as the exuberance of actuality beyond the circle of potencies for Schelling), but as releasement and abandonment (*Gelassenheit*) of the law of the concept: to exist is to be released open, and to abandon the law of the concept. Existence breaks through the mythic circle of potencies that constitutes the power, force and the gaze of the law, and makes it 'dance nimbly in the service of thought' (Kierkegaard 2009a: 87).

> I have only my own life, which I offer as soon as a difficulty appears. Then the dance is easy, because my partner is the thought of death, and it is a lively dancer. People are too heavy for me, therefore I request *per deos obsecro*: no one invite me, because I will not dance. (Ibid.)

As in Nietzsche, thinking is here dancing – and not the ponderous mobility of cognitive categories of Hegel – whose partner is death. To exist is to bring together, in the intimacy of existing, 'thinking' and 'death': it is always the thought of death which opens, simultaneously, to what does not terminate itself in any finality of death. As if the immense movement of the 'dizzying dialectic', with all its mobile cognitive categories, has to come to its standstill, to the momentary arrest of its mobility – which is the instance of death – to open to another, new and qualitatively heterogeneous 'becoming' where the concept dies, and existence is *spaced* open to the infinity of faith. Thus, this mortification, which is the dance of existence 'in the service of truth', is also transmutation and transfiguration: something new comes into being; something else happens which the law of the concept (*Begriff*) cannot grasp (*greifen*); as something which is qualitatively heterogeneous from the order of the law, something that sets itself *apart* from the control of *hegemonikon* and from any of its legitimating function: it is the *interruption* or a radical *insurrection* (*stasis*) of the mythic foundation of any hegemonic regime. In this sense, this *breakthrough* is truly *historical*, in the sense of a new inauguration which cannot be axiomatically deduced from any principle (*arché*), from any hypothesis or doctrine, from any theorem or logical premise: its ground is the abyss of freedom. The leap of dance leaps from, and through, and over this abyss, making all immanent transition of one category to the other, of one potency to the other, impossible. This impossible is the impossibility of death over which the leap leaps. Kierkegaard calls this impossible 'paradox'. It is the peril of the impassable aporia through which, over which, knowledge passes into faith, and then one is born anew: 'the deadly peril of lying upon the 70,000 fathom, only there to find God' (Kierkegaard 2009b: 195).

As existence is the releasement and abandonment of the violence of the law – a dancing – so faith for Kierkegaard is the releasement and abandonment of the violence of cognitive mastery. The originary violence of metaphysics is this cognitive violence that the concept imposes upon the Adamic naming of truth in order to subsume the singularity of the phenomenon. 'Probably few fields of study', writes Kierkegaard in his diary,

> bestow on man the serene and happy frame of mind that the natural sciences give him. Out into nature he goes, everything is familiar, it is as though he had talked with the plants and the animals beforehand. He sees not only the uses man can put them to (for that is quite secondary) but their significance in the whole universe. He stands like Adam of old – all the animals come to him and he gives them names. (Kierkegaard 1996: 14)

The concepts in the immense system don't give *the truth of the way* but rather they chatter interminably and incessantly: they prattle away, submerging the truth of the singular into the formless swarm of the homogenous multitudes: 'chatter is the absolute downfall of every spiritual state of affairs' (Kierkegaard 2009b: 417). Kierkegaard finds the violence of this prattle to be the very emblematic of the violence of his contemporary world of modernity: the anonymous order of totality that flattens away the irreducible singularity and the non-identical into the homogenous and empty meaning that he calls 'the crowd', a homogeneous massification, an empty universality where there is no actuality, a tyrannical order of hegemony where everyone acts like a monarch for his or her self-interest.

This hegemonic order of tyranny is metaphysically reflected in the 'dizzying dialectic' of Hegel: all concepts are mediated; all transition is a mediation, a homogenous continuum; and all that the concept grasps is nothing other than what already belongs to the infinite web of reason. The infinitude that this dialectic opens up is dizzying: formless, measureless, quantitative entities multiplied to infinity, for infinity itself is only a category. Here, at least till here, Kierkegaardian 'deconstruction' of the 'dizzying dialectic' of Hegel is still, more or less, Schellingian: that existence must be absolved from the tyranny of the 'dizzying dialectic' which, in the social order of the world, is reflected in the order of totality of the modern epoch: quantification of the individual, particularisation of the singular, and totalisation of the social existence into a homogeneous mass. What rules here, as in the 'dizzying dialectic' of Hegelian panlogicism, is the principle of immanence and autochthony: the apocalyptic sting of the outside, of the imminent and yet incalculable eschatological heterogeneity, is being secularised and neutralised; the result is the mythic order of totality which is dizzying to the gaze, for it opens up to nothing, an order of the world where anonymity denudes all that is singular and irreducible:

> Spiritually understood, dizziness may have a double character. It may be occasioned by the fact that a man has so wandered astray in the infinite that nothing finite can acquire for him substantial existence, that he can get no standard of measurement. This kind of dizziness consists rather in an excess of imagination, and inasmuch as one might conceive of dizziness metaphorically with relation to the eye, one might perhaps call it single-sighted dizziness. The other kind of dizziness is produced by an abstract dialectic, owing to the fact that it sees absolutely everything double, sees nothing at all. This kind of dizziness one might call double-sighted dizziness. Salvation from all dizziness, spiritually understood, is essentially to seek the ethical, which by qualitative dialectic disciplines and limits the individual and establishes his task. (Kierkegaard 1994: 221–2)

In that way, the very possibility of an eschatological judgement upon the violence of this anonymous totality of history has been taken away by the secularising project of modernity. In this dizzying dialectic of 'the present age' all individuation is swallowed by the overwhelming power of empty universality – the crowd, the public, the anonymous totality of world-history – as if sucked up into a black night where 'all cows are black' (Hegel 1977: 9). This is, in a way, to turn Hegel against himself in a Schellingian way. It is the 'dizzying dialectic' of the speculative philosopher who paints the world, which already for him is over, grey upon grey.

It is against this dizzying world painted grey upon grey that Kierkegaard invokes the *spacing* of existence: *the space of the world* must be *spaced-open*; not only that time is to be released from the horizon of space (which is understood as extension in the dominant metaphysics) but that space of the world itself must be *temporalised*. Only the *temporalising space* – which Kierkegaard calls here 'spacing' – where space becomes the open of *distensio*, where (which is 'nowhere', not a specific space but the *coming* of space, the exposing open of the universal to the eschatological singular to come) an interruption opens up, there manifests – outside the 'constituted order of phenomenality' (Schürmann): *Existenz*. Hence existence each time for Kierkegaard manifests itself as 'inter-esse': the 'interest' of existence manifests itself as 'inter-esse'. The actuality of existence 'is an interesse splitting the hypothetical unity of abstraction's thought and being. Abstraction deals with possibility and actuality, but the grasp of actuality gives a false account, since the medium is not actuality but possibility . . .' (Kierkegaard 2009b: 263).

The logic of the concept, when the concept is made mobile (as in Hegel), is that of passing from possibility into actuality: Aristotle as much as Hegel names this as 'movement'. But it is a hypothetical existence whose medium is still only possibility, while the actuality *as* actuality – of existence – is not a 'passing' of a categorical movement but a transition as *leap*. *The leap*, thus, can't belong to the hypothetical unity of thought and being; it is 'as break, yes, as a suffering' (ibid.: 278). The *spacing* that brings the *disparate* together (singular-universal, mortality-natality, destitution-institution) while *setting apart*, is the suffering of the *leap* that holds together the disjunctive 'either/or', not in the hypothetical-categorical unity of an immanent movement that is dizzying to the intellect, but in the qualitative dialectic that, by introducing the eschatological justice that interrupts, 'disciplines and limits' the empty universal and salvages us from 'the dizzying dialectic'. What puts into question the tyranny of the dizzying dialectic (whose reflection in the objective-social world is the modern *hegemonikon* of the public and the crowd) is the eschatological justice that is ethico-religious event par excellence: it is this that interests existence, *existence* which each time is singular, absolved from the empty generality, whose image of language is not prattle but the Adamic language of the name. It is this purity of the name that alone bears the promise and the fulfilment of an eschatological beatitude, while here in the profane order of earthly existence it manifests itself as *judgement* that *spaces* the world *apart* from its deepest foundation.

Existence spaces open the 'esse' (hence it occurs as 'inter-esse': in-between of 'esse'). Though eschatologically oriented to the beatific truth in the glowing light of redemption, on the profane-earthly order existence always appears as suffering: the leap – which is not movement – is suffering.

The Occidental metaphysics determines 'becoming' on the basis of movement. Thus Hegel's 'onto-theological constitution of metaphysics' too – which makes even concepts mobile – understands 'becoming' on the basis of movement. On the other hand, Kierkegaard releases *becoming* from 'the dizzying dialectic' of movement (in which sense, yet again, Kierkegaard remains close to the later Schelling), and hence, in his own fashion, thinks outside metaphysics: existence is not given being, not even the pure being with which the speculative logic begins (and then immanently passes over into *nothing*, and then to *becoming* as the synthesis of being and nothing), but *becoming* that leaps over the abyss of the moment. One can see here why *the leap does not belong to the movement*. The leap opens existence from the overwhelming tyranny of the anonymous order of empty universality to the singularity of the future, the 'singularity to come' (Reiner Schürmann). The singular individual who is singularised by death ('my partner is the thought of death, and it is a lively dancer') is absolved from the totality of the general order by virtue of the ethico-religious suffering that s/he undergoes:

> Ethics concentrates on the individual, and ethically it is the task of every individual to become a whole human being; just as it is the ethical presupposition that everyone is born in the state of being able to become one. (Kierkegaard 2009b: 290)

'To become one' what one is: this is not the requirement of 'the dizzying dialectic'; what 'the dizzying dialectic' requires is that the singular individual submits himself or herself to the force of the law, subsumes herself or himself to the gaze of the concept. This is why we need a qualitative dialectic, the dialectic of infinity, in which the singular subjective thinker 'has the passion of thought needed to keep hold of the qualitative disjunction . . . the absolute disjunction, belonging as it does to existence is something that the subjective thinker has, with the passion of thought, but he has it as the final decision that ensures that not everything ends up in a quantifying' (ibid.: 294). Thus, it belongs to the logic of the qualitative dialectic that the eschatological beatitude and divine glory has to appear on the earthly order as *suffering*: the divine pleroma, when it becomes to manifest in the earthly order only to tear the totalised order of constituted phenomenality, it has to appear itself as equal to zero! Later, Kierkegaard would draw out all the theologico-political consequences of this qualitative dialectic whose single task is to single out and release, through mortification and suffering that involves in 'transition as leap', the element of singularity from the violence of the world-historical reason. Unlike Hegelian 'dizzying dialectic' that finds in the objective order of the Prussian state the *figuration* of the Absolute Spirit, Kierkegaard's qualitative-eschatological dialectic, the true Absolute – the divine pleroma – becomes disfigured and unrecognisable: *the Christ kept hanging on the cross*!

This is why *suffering* is the heart of ethics and religion. Suffering is the fundamental attunement of ethico-religious existence, while in the aesthetic-immanent sphere of 'the dizzying dialectic' suffering can only be an accidental occurrence, a provisional even though necessary, diremption in sight of its *Aufhebung* into self-presence. The melancholy dialectic of Kierkegaard, like the melancholy dialectic of Benjamin, is not the dialectic that is satisfied to remember the 'gallery of images'(Hegel 1977: 492) that the world has become, but the dialectic that salvages the element of singularity that is threatened to disappear in the anonymous night of the empty universal. This element appears – suddenly, in a momentary manner, as the sudden moment – as *the disjunctive simultaneity*, as sudden eruption in the midst of continuity, as arresting of the movement of continuum. What Benjamin calls 'Now-Time' is 'the moment' for Kierkegaard; 'to unite the moments of life in simultaneity, just that is the task' (Kierkegaard 2009b: 292). As the existential moment of the subjective thinker, it is 'passion' which is 'the tensing in the contradiction' such that what is eschatologically joy is here and now grasped as melancholy, what is the eschatological eternity – in absolute disjunction from time – is grasped *hic et nunc* as the abyss of the moment (ibid.: 326). Therefore, the qualitative dialectic can only be an indirect expression of the absolute, because it is always 'on the way' – it is *the way* – which, by an irreducible disjunction, *spaces open* the 'esse' of existence. What Kierkegaard means by 'becoming' is not the Absolute Spirit that speculatively falls into the temporal-historical process, but this *spacing-open* of the *esse* of existence. Becoming is not a process; Kierkegaardian becoming is not the world-historical becoming of Hegel that teleologically moves ahead on a continuous plane of immanence. The *temporality of the spacing* – of existence – is not an instantiation of the universal, homogeneous, empty time: *spacing* does not belong to time; it does not occur *in* time; it is the abyss of the moment that holds together the absolute disjunction simultaneously, and arrests the dizzying movement of the quantitative dialectic, and brings it to a standstill. The moment of arrest is a wrenching – 'the wrench of decision' (ibid.) – which renews existence and redeems itself from the violence of the world-historical reason, from the violence of the totalitarian order of constituted phenomenality.

De-cision, then, is intrinsic to existence: *spacing* not only holds the disparate together but keeps the disparate *as* disparate, without any dialectical-aesthetic mediation. The event of the *spacing* – of existence – must not, then, be thought of as the unitary ground of an aesthetic-immanent dialectic, as mere transition belonging to an immanent movement, but as de-cision (*decidere*: cision, cutting off, separating) of existence that transforms everything: 'the existing person changes everything in his existence in relation to the highest good' (ibid.: 327). This transformation of existence in the *spacing* of *de-cision* – dancing itself – releases existence from the mythic law of necessity (where the possibility ever returns into the same) and places it in radical freedom. De-cision, which for Kierkegaard is always the decision for faith, tears out and spaces open the fabric of natural ties of the aesthetic sphere of life (which is governed by the mythic law of necessity, and which is apotheosised in 'the dizzying dialectic' of empty infinity), and *spaces* existence in the open region of freedom. A tragic freedom it is, for here the disparate – the qualitative disjunction between the singular and the universal, the God and man, eternity and time – is not resolved into the higher synthesis of (dizzying) dialectical mediation: the singular, the subjective thinker, who is decided by faith by the virtue of the paradox (which is incommensurable to analogy and to any dialectical mediation), is *ubique et nusquam* (everywhere and nowhere), like the Archimedean point, the radical outside of all totality and all possible enclosures. Here thinking becomes dancing whose partner is none other than death; here the grim seriousness of the concept, with all its patience and ponderousness, gives way to the inner gaiety of nimble playing and dancing (for the subjective thinker earnest and jest are twine sisters).

Playing-spacing here is neither to be understood as the aesthetic play of appearances belonging to the cognitive subject of experience, nor is it to be understood as the cosmic play of immanent-natural life: neither the aesthetic play of appearances nor the cosmic-natural life are impervious to the grasping violence of 'the dizzying dialectic'. 'The dizzying dialectic' of empty infinity allows the aesthetic play of appearances and the idea of the play of natural life only so as to subsume them under the mythic violence of the concept where the law of necessity rules sovereign. In the realm of theology, the play of the cosmic-natural life often degenerates into the mythic-pantheistic *auto-poesis*: the abyss of the *distance* between the divine and the mortal, and the qualitative disjunction between eternity and time are, then, dialectically mediated into the hypothetical unity of *pan-theos*. The tragic event of *spacing* – which is the event par excellence – is, then, at once denied: de-cision that is borne out of the abyss of freedom is made impossible; and responsibility of the mortal to keep the world open to its radical futurity (by keeping the abyss of the distance open) is *always already* foreclosed. This is the *arché-violence* of 'the dizzying dialectic' against which we must bring into *insurrection* and *resurrection*, so Kierkegaard would say, the redeeming-eschatological violence of the ethico-religious which alone therapeutically cures us from the giddy infinity of the quantitative dialectic.

This is why we need to have more than one sphere of life, not successively but simultaneously, holding the absolute disparate together, and yet holding them as disparate, without any dialectical mediation. For Kierkegaard, aesthetic-ethico-religious are not three successive spheres of life through which the subjective thinker progressively passes towards a determinate goal, following a certain logic of linear progression. To think the stages of life that way is to write another 'phenomenology of spirit': the linear movement of life, necessarily progressive, determines becoming on the basis of movement, and subsumes the incalculable, radical breaks into the fold of an immanent, hypothetical unity of thought and being (as in Hegel). To think the spheres of life as successive is to deny the moment its chance of its eschatological eruption in the midst of time: the moment when the radical *turning* and *converting* takes place; when at the abyss of the *moment* eternity suddenly enters into time, and interrupts the continuum of historical progression, and when existence becomes as new as this now: 'Behold, I make all things new' (Revelation 21: 5). 'To make all things new', God himself must interrupt and introduce an abyss of *distance* between Him and the world, *breaking apart* and *setting apart* any possible hypothetical unity of pantheism: the ethico-religious is this suspension of the mythic law of the world, of the natural-cosmic life where necessity and fate rule as the sovereign master. In the natural-aesthetic life fate strikes with the mythic violence of the law; the ethico-religious, on the other hand, salvages us from 'the dizzying dialectic' of the concept by *spacing* the world open. The world is *spaced* open by the absolute paradox (that God actually becomes one single individual, and not man as such) without mediation. That this *paradox* has occurred once, this absolute historical event that has also disjoined the profane history *apart*: this certainty can never be reached by the hypothetical dialectical mediation and speculative knowledge. It only belongs to the madness and absurdity of faith for the subjective thinker who has introduced, in his or her own existence, the ethico-religious *spacing* of existence by virtue of an impossible *de-cision*. Thus, *spacing* of existence is for Kierkegaard the religious problematic par excellence: the *turning* or *converting* which alone transfigures the sickness of 'the dizzying dialectic' into the redemptive truth of the way ('I am the way, the truth and the life'; John 16: 6) is the very impossible possibility of faith, faith as radical actuality and not as a hypothetic-conceptual possibility. What, then, *spaces* existence open is not an inherent, natural and intrinsic possibility immanent in the natural-cosmic-aesthetic life: it is rather the absolute heterogeneity of faith, inaccessible to any human possibility or capacity, whether that of knowledge or of action. Neither any theological or philosophical doctrine (whether theory of being or theory of knowledge) nor any human work merits this advent of faith. By putting into question the very legitimacy of the human capacity and possibility, faith's *spacing* conjures up the impossible event of existence.

Phenomenology of destitution

What Kierkegaard calls 'the stages of life' is not to be understood as the speculative-dialectical stages leading to the absolute identity via the mediation of the third stage, but as stages which, each time and singularly, manifest the disparate *as* disparate: the tragic disparate pierces through all mediation, and manifests itself as suffering. Thus the 'transition' between the stages of life – between the aesthetic and the ethical, and between the ethical and the religious – is not an immanent transition on a homogenous scale but each time is a piercing *phenomenalising* of an irreducible and abyssal contradiction which expresses itself either as *irony* (as between the aesthetic and the ethical) or as *humour* (as between the ethical and the religious). Such an eschatological 'phenomenology' of Kierkegaard is truly a phenomenology of 'spirit': phenomenology as intensification of difference; phenomenology as exposure to the extreme moment of existence where the subjective thinker, at the exception of all normative situations and at the limit of knowledge, confronts the decision of faith. The religious is indeed the manifestation of the Absolute, as in Hegel (for whom the religious is the manifestation of the absolute as absolute in its immediate form), but this manifestation, for the subjective thinker, is not the self-presence of the Absolute in its intelligibility and luminosity, but precisely is the manifestation of the scandal – of the absolute paradox: that the Absolute has to manifest itself as incognito and unrecognisable, in the form of the servant, utterly destitute and weak. 'We have eaten and drunk in thy presence', Kierkegaard quotes from Luke, 'and thou hast taught in our streets . . . I know you not whence ye are' (13: 26–7).

Here, then, unlike the Hegelian phenomenology of spirit, is the phenomenology of destitution and weakness of sovereignty: the spirit is destitution par excellence. What Kierkegaard calls 'deepening of inwardness' is not the interiorising-spiritual work of exteriority (and vice versa) and upliftment, through negation (*Aufheben*), of the given world in self-recognising cognition, but is an intensification of spirit that is at once a destitution – or weakening – of the spirit. Here, Kierkegaard closely follows – and Dietrich Bonhoeffer will do the same nearly a century later – the fundamental teaching of the Sermon of the Mount: 'Blessed *are* the poor in spirit: for theirs is the kingdom of heaven' (Matthew 5: 3). The spirit discloses itself, phenomenalises itself or manifests itself, in and as destitution. The exception of spirit – and spirit is exception, and lies at the extreme limit of all cognition and normative situations of human possibilities – is not the exception of a sovereign power; it is rather the exception of a disclosure where all the attributes, predicates or qualities of the worldly-natural existence become like 'Christ becoming the servant': here it is not the *Aufhebung* that is the sovereign principle of the Absolute Knowledge but *kenosis* as the phenomenological disclosure of utter destitution of sovereignty. If the religious, for Kierkegaard, is the extreme limit of existence, it is not because it is the *telos* of existence where existence rounds itself off and forms its closure and fulfilment in reconciliation. The extreme limit of the religious is rather a manifestation of a *dis-enclosure* where totality comes to its sudden halt and is exposed open to the absolute *disparate as disparate*, where knowledge suffers in paradox, where all human merit and capacity hangs on the cross, and time becomes the empty measure of eternity. But this empty measure of time is also the fullness of time where *kenosis* coincides with glory (which is the absolute paradox!): 'But when the time had finally come', Kierkegaard cites from Galatians 4: 4, 'God has sent forth his son'. It is not that this coincidence takes away the disparate *as* disparate; it is not 'the hypothetical unity of thought and being'. Rather, this *coincidence* is also the revelation of the absolute *disjunction* that makes all synthesis and all possible totality in knowledge impossible: where eternity breaks through time and overcomes it, this moment – empty and full at the same instance – is also the moment of absolute disjunction. The advent of the Son tears apart the fabric of time and separates the world from its foundation: no 'hypothetical unity of being and thought' renders it present and makes it a presence in the world. It does away with any possible analogy of beings. The world-historical movement of progress (which is also, as Walter Benjamin reminds us, only the triumphal story of the spoils of civilisation getting passed from one victor to another) here loses its power of soliciting 'normative obligations' (Schürmann 2003) from us.

The moment suspends all determinacy that constitutes the law of necessity. The Kierkegaardian moment has the biblical *Kairos* character here: the moment is the moment of the *turn*, of conversion, of total transfiguration of 'esse'. This turn does not take place without breaking the 'esse' from its hypothetical unity to thought. The *Kairos*-turn is the exceptional turn – the turn of the exception – from the hegemonic fantasm of the totalising universal towards the 'singularization to come' (ibid.). The Kierkegaardian phenomenology of the disparate discloses this turn, this crossroad, this inter-section (also disjunction) where the religious happens, and faith occurs as grace by suspending the necessity and determinacy that governs the logic of the concept and the power of the law. Though there is a turn from aesthetic stage to the ethical – and this transition too is a kind of a leap (which is dramatised by irony; Socrates is the master of irony) – the religious (because it is spirit and spiritual) is the true turn; it is indeed the true leap and the true break par excellence: from the mythic immanent life into the *historical*, from the necessity and determinacy of the past into the abyssal *freedom* of the future, from the hegemonic fantasm of the totalising universal to the '*singularization* to come'. The moment releases (by abandoning the law of the world, by making it inoperative) the trait of singularity (which always is 'to come') from being enclosed in the natural life of the aesthetic sphere where the concept strikes with the force of fate, where singulars are reduced to particulars and are subsumed to the anonymous order of totality.

The abyss of the moment

It is in *Philosophical Fragments* that Kierkegaard sets forth the Pauline eschatological moment against the Platonic Greek-mythical conception: the moment as the *turn* that *restitutes in integrum* the originary freedom. This unthinkable paradox, which is the vertigo for thought, that the abyss of the moment is at once the *pleroma* of time, is the decisive – where decision is to be made (*decidere*: to cut off, to bring into cision) – turning point of existence to the religious: the moment turns, while interrupting, the circle of time from error to *truth*, from bondage to *freedom*, from life under the mythic violence of the law to the redemptive violence *love*. The one who has chosen, out of the abyss of freedom, bondage, and thereby self-cancelling that freedom (which for Kierkegaard is the state of sin) – if he or she were to be given that moment again to choose otherwise, which is 'impossible', that moment would transfigure his or her whole existence. This absolute moment, which is 'impossible' each time – for it restitutes the condition that has, as it were, immemorially passed – is, paradoxically, the very fullness of time. The moment, in all its 'impossibility', is not mere absence of time but its plenitude in its very destitution: the moment is rather the very event of time. The moment would, then, no longer belong to the homogeneous empty scale of time, as though it were a mere particular instantiation of an empty universality; rather, the ecstasy of the moment is the very event of existence. It completely transforms the person: 'we become a different person, not in the factious sense of becoming another of the same quality, but a qualitatively different person, or as we will call it, a new person' (Kierkegaard 2009a: 96).

This is why the moment has the decisive existential importance: the event of existence turns at and as the decision of the moment. But the moment is precisely the 'impossible' par excellence: how is it possible that the moment can be given again (because it has immemorially passed by to a past before any passed past), for only if it were possible the individual can be born anew, and can be made whole? This idea, which is the decisively eschatological moment in the biblical discourse ('Behold, I make all things new'), is the very idea of the *impossible*: it goes against all doxa, and all understanding. And yet without this impossibly paradoxical event, a paradox which is 'the scandal for the Jews and foolishness for the Greeks' (1 Corinthians 1: 23), existence would remain enclosed in the cages of the law and its necessity: the past decision for bondage (which as cancellation of the originary freedom is the state of sin) would remain determinate for all eternity, and no redemption would ever atone the guilt in any time to come. If redemption were to be possible, not only is the individual to be given the truth (the new truth, which is not the truth of the world) but even the condition of reception of that truth must also be given. This means nothing other than the very possibility of restitution of the originary freedom in the moment, once again: only this impossible possibility can decisively disrupt the vicious circle of the guilt and punishment, can interrupt the vicious economy of the law, and the power of the past over us. Redemption, then, which always is freedom *from* the violence of fate (therefore is freedom par excellence), cannot be thought as mere recollection of the past which has always been with us as our potentiality but is to be understood as the impossible restitution of that immemorial which makes everything new.

This is why the Platonic-Greek-philosophical conception of recollection is insufficient for our redemption: 'while Greek pathos is concentrated on recollection, the pathos of our project is concentrated on the moment' (Kierkegaard 2009a: 98). The Platonic conception of recollection is based upon the logic of possibility: it is a possibility given in the intra-mundane and inter-human relationships in the earthly order as the highest possibility. That the occasion of learning and the occasioned can correspond in our recollection is a potentiality which always and already is given to us: this is the highest human possibility. But here the moment loses its decisive significance; it is 'instantly swallowed up by recollection' (ibid.: 106). Since the condition of recollection is already there, and it is only the matter of bringing it into manifestation, it can't free us from the determinacy of the past condition and can't wholly transfigure our existence.

On the other hand, if the moment is to have decisive significance for the mortal, the condition of receiving the truth must not be given to him or her as his or her possibility; it must be created or made born, which God alone can do.

The moment, then, cannot be incorporated into the logic of correspondence (between the occasioned and the occasion); rather, the moment wholly exposes us to the abyss of non-correspondence and the incommensurable and the impossible: 'the moment appears precisely in the relation between the eternal resolution and the incommensurable occasion' (ibid.: 101). That eternity arrives in time, or that eternity breaks through time: this can neither be understood on the basis of analogy nor on the basis of the logic of correspondence. The infinite and incommensurable *distance* marked by the abyss of the absolute disjunction can't be traversed by any *analogia* or correspondence. How, then, can the truth and also the condition of receiving the truth (which is neither a worldly truth nor the truth of the world) be given? It can't be given in recollection.

The irreducible distance can be equalled – in the abyss of the moment when it arrives in time – only in love. *God has to abandon all his sovereign power, and renounce the divine force, and descend to the lowliest out of love*: 'Thus God will reveal himself in the form of a servant' (ibid.: 106).

> And this is the omnipotence of the decisive love, to be able to do what neither the king nor Socrates were able to do and which is the reason that their assumed forms were really a kind of deception. (Ibid.: 107)

The power of divine love is the *kenosis* of all mythic power. The glory of love is the form of the lowliest: 'thus the God is on earth like unto the lowliest through his omnipotent love' (ibid.). The omnipotence of love is *im-potentia*: this absolute paradox can't be understood by Socratic pathos but by the Christian eschatological intensity of the heart. With the arrival of *Love*, the force of judgement is rendered null. This making null – this suffering of the break – is not the accidental property of love; it is what love itself must be on the earthly order: suffering belongs to love as the very possibility of manifestation of love on the earthly order.

> But the servant form was not a costume. The God must, therefore, suffer everything, endure everything, hunger in the desert, thirst in anguish, be forsaken in death that is his suffering, the whole of this life is a story of suffering, and it is love that suffers, love that grieves everything which is itself needy. (Ibid.)

The Kierkegaardian phenomenology is not the phenomenology of the Subject that undergoes suffering – 'the pathway ... of despair' (Hegel 1977: 49) – only to sublate it on the cross into the absolute form of reconciliation as Absolute Knowledge. The Kierkegaardian phenomenology is rather a paradoxical phenomenology, the phenomenology of paradox that exposes us to the absolute heterogeneity and the unknown, to that absolute *difference* that 'cannot be pinned down' by the power of the concept (Kierkegaard 2009a: 117). What this phenomenology manifests is not 'the hypothetical unity of thought and being' but the immeasurable distance of actuality, the qualitative *distance* that is at once diachronic and infinite: 'the understanding has got God as close as possible, and yet He remains as far away as ever' (ibid.: 118). This releasing of God 'beyond esse', which is an exuberant actuality beyond any potentiality, is the project that Kierkegaard shares with the late Schelling against the Hegelian subsumption of actuality into the immanent movement of possibility (Kierkegaard) or potentiality (Schelling): in each case the political eschatology is bound up with this deconstructive gesture of opening God beyond various metaphysical closures of onto-theology. The irreducible disjunction and this abyss of heterogeneity, which no theologico-political principle of analogy can bridge, cannot be mediated by any speculative knowledge, even if it is Absolute Knowledge, and cannot be accessed by any force of the concept: love alone – who is Love – by renouncing the violence of the sovereign power, can participate in the truth which, being unconditional and surpassingly generous, pours itself over creaturely existence, and redeems it from the violence of the profane order (where sovereign power rules over life by force). This is why both Schelling (as early as his essay on human freedom of 1809) and Kierkegaard replace the dialectical violence of the Absolute Concept with the un-pre-thinkable abyss of Love who outpours himself on our earthly being; He who has renounced, through mortification, all attributes of sovereignty. The Christological centrality of this political eschatology is here unmistakable: because this divine love (which ecstatically precedes even the distinction between good and evil) is in absolute dissymmetry in respect to all worldly *potestas*, it can only appear on the profane order as the *paradox* which is offensive. The unconditional affirmation of pure love, in all its pure generosity, can only manifest on the profane order as an absolute negativity: suffering on the cross that is inhospitable and intolerable. What the paradox points towards, that is, to the pure affirmation of beatitude or glorious resurrection, can only appear on the order of the world as the eschatological event: the event yet *to come*, the new inauguration at the end of the world!

The unconditional demand of eschatological redemption, then, needs the *paradox* of the moment: 'the moment is the paradox' (ibid.: 128). The Socratic pathos does not recognise the significance of the moment and the paradox because it does not recognise the unconditional demand of redemption. In that sense, according to Kierkegaard, the Hegelian pathos of recollection (of 'the gallery of images' at the dusk of world-history) inhabits in the same pantheist-immanent metaphysics as the Socratic recollection: only by way of an exit (*Ausgang*) from that metaphysics can the problematic of religion be thinkable for the subjective thinker. In that sense Kierkegaard's eschatological religion is similar, and yet opposed to, Marx's atheistic *Ausgang* (Löwith 1991; Bensussan 2007): that (Hegelian) metaphysics needs to be exited, but the actual equality cannot be attained through the medium of intra-mundane and inter-human politics. That politics cannot have for the mortal the absolute significance and ultimate meaning: this theologico-political opening up of religion, beyond politics, that opens Kierkegaard for Rosenzweig and Lévinas (for Lévinas, this beyond of political ontology is understood as the ethical infinity) of our time. This is why the Kierkegaardian question of the 'moment' (which for Rosenzweig is the messianic problematic par excellence), and the Kierkegaardian emphasis upon 'singularity', which is absolved from totality, are of decisive importance for Rosenzweig: once 'the moment' gets intensified and singularity is released – the singularity of the individual who faces death *as* death – then the triumphal march of the world-historical politics loses the significance of the absolute. The absolute of the world-historical movement, where the violence and tyranny of the historical reason itself remains unquestioned, then becomes reduced to the relativities and conditionality of the intra-mundane and inter-human politics.

The moment, then, acquires for Kierkegaard – and for Rosenzweig, though in a different manner – an eschatological resonance: the absolute negativity of the paradox (that it does not manifest itself in the profane-worldly order in its pure affirmation and beatitude but as suffering) has the character of judgement about it. The 'No' of negativity – of the paradox – is the 'No' thrown at the face of the world-Historical reason, a passionate refusal to participate in the triumphal march of the world-historical politics. This is why Christ, whose Kingdom is not the kingdom of the world, is a scandal and foolishness. This dissymmetry marks each moment in Christ's own life: 'eternity is swaddled in the news of the day', for 'the news of the day is the beginning of eternity' (Kierkegaard 2009a: 128). The moment, then, cannot be understood world-historically: to follow Christ, to be a Christian, is to let this abyss appear in each individual's own existence in the middle of world-historical triumph. The moment is the cry of suffering in the battleground of the world-historical triumph. This suffering of the moment, rising against the triumphal cry of world-historical politics, belongs to faith alone, uniquely to the religious sphere of existence.

The moment, then, does not belong as one moment among others to the world-historical movement which the speculative Spirit undertakes: the moment absolves itself, as does the singularity, from the anonymous order of totality. The moment is singular; the moment is the event of the singular existence, existence which each time is singular. For both Kierkegaard and Rosenzweig, the point of departure is to think the moment as the thought of death. It is not the death which is the work of the law; it is rather the death when the work of the law becomes inoperative. In the regime of the law, and in the order of the concept, the singular is incorporated into totality by the labour of negativity: the law strikes the individual's mere life in the way that the force of fate strikes on the guilty individual. Death here appears either as the medium of incorporation into the universal order of the concept, or as punishment of a retributive justice. But there is another 'experience' of death when the moment becomes the moment of inoperation – of the work of the law, of the law of the concept. This is the point of departure for Rosenzweig's great *The Star of Redemption*, and this is also the point of departure for Kierkegaard's eschatological vision of eternity: the arrival of eternity in time – which is the moment – is the inoperation of the law, and suspension of the concept. The moment is the point of departure to the coming establishment of the divine kingdom, but here and now, *hic et nunc*, the moment is the destitution and mortification of all establishment. However, in Rosenzweig's messianic religion the apocalyptic sting is minimised, while in Kierkegaard's eschatology the apocalyptic sting of judgement is intensified and is named as 'the fourth state'. In both cases, existence means being outside the anonymous and tyrannical order of totality: eschatological or messianic existence as 'being-with'. In the coming Kingdom of God there is all life, but it has to take death as the point of departure in the unredeemed world. This is why in Kierkegaard, as much as in Rosenzweig, the redemptive consummation of history is life in eternity, a redeemed life, but its point of departure is always the irreducible experience of death *as* death.

If redemption were to be possible for the singular being unto death, then the moment has to be released from the law of the concept, and from the logic of necessity. *Philosophical Fragments* which is still a 'philosophical' book – and it talks like a book (Jünger 2014) – philosophically attempts to release the non-necessity of the event from the logic of movement: to say that the moment does not belong to (let's say 'Hegelian') movement is to say that the event of redemption arrives out of the abyssal freedom (which is not a human possibility); and that it is not an intra-mundane world-historical occurrence. Whether in Socratic recollection, or in Hegelian recollection, the non-necessity of redemption (via absurdity of the paradox) is foreclosed; and freedom, which is the abyssal ground of history, becomes unthinkable. In this profound sense, Christianity is the *historical* event par excellence: 'everything that has come to be *eo ipso* historical'; 'the decisive predicate of history is that it has come to be' (Kierkegaard 2009a: 143). In the rigorous sense, nature has no history, because nature has no dialectical relationship with time. History, on the other hand,

> Contain[s] a re-doubling – i.e. the possibility of another becoming within its original becoming. Here is the historical in the stricter sense which is dialectical with respect to time. The becoming that is here the same as the becoming of nature is a possibility, a possibility that is nature's whole actuality. But the genuine historical becoming takes place within a becoming, this must be remembered. The more specific historical becoming comes to be through a relatively freely acting cause, which always definitely points back to an absolutely freely acting cause. (Ibid.: 143–4)

If the possibility of another becoming 'within a becoming' – this re-doubling which Kierkegaard calls 'dialectical' – defines the event of the historical, then it must be predicated upon freedom: a *turn*, a radical *break* or a quantum *leap* must be possible in the manner of 'non-necessity' (that something wholly otherwise comes to pass); the leap that cannot be mere transition within an immanent movement of concepts, however mobile they may be. The moment, then, comes to be through an inscrutable freedom, a freedom through which something that is impossible otherwise may, nevertheless, come to pass. This moment, in the manner of 'non-necessity', brings to a sudden pause the whole teleological movement, and brings into being that which is outside of that movement. The moment, then, is *historical* event, and yet precisely thereby it can't be understood purely (world) historically:

> Christianity is the only historical phenomenon that despite the historical, has wished to be the point of departure for the individual's eternal consciousness, has wished to interest him in another way than purely historically, has wished to base his eternal happiness on his relation to something historical. (Ibid.: 172)

The moment, because it is the event of non-necessity, cannot be reached teleologically through historical reason, and is therefore not a (world) 'historical' phenomenon; and yet, it is *historical* in a more originary sense: that it lets the event of coming to come via the impossible, that eternity may at all arrive in time, that a new inauguration may at all happen within 'a becoming'. That something or someone may arrive which cannot be anticipated or programmatically calculated beforehand – which therefore is the *coming* par excellence – this un-programmable and incalculable event, this purely unconditional arrival, is to be thought outside the pantheistic-immanent metaphysics of Hegel. By introducing this tear, which is the tear of faith, *Philosophical Fragments* tears up once more 'the hypothetical unity' of faith and knowledge (which Hegel thought he had reconciled on a speculative Good Friday): the abyss once more opens up between the profane order of world-historical triumph and that absolutely historical event when all triumph is abandonment on the night of the cross: 'a triumphant faith is incomparably ridiculous' (ibid.: 171). Philosophically though, Kierkegaard here replaces the Hegelian triumph of *Weltgeschichte* with the mystery of suffering (which is the secret of religious faith). Faith has nothing to do with triumph in the profane order: while its triumph is elsewhere, in the order of the world it is all suffering and destitution.

Divine madness

While in the pathos of recollection the singularity is swallowed up (in its most triumphant form it assumes the metaphysical totalisation of onto-theology), the decision of faith is an eternal affirmation of faith which can only appear in the triumphant order of world-historical progress as *martyrdom*. *Concluding Unscientific Postscript* draws out all the decisive theologico-political consequences of this affirmation that Johannes Climacus (Kierkegaard) sets out in *Philosophical Fragments*. At work here is a certain 'deconstruction' of historical Reason that the dominant metaphysical order of totality assumes. The decision of faith, because its affirmation can only manifest itself as martyrdom – 'faith's martyrdom' (Kierkegaard 2009b: 28) – is thus a 'divine madness': 'I must learn in my God-relationship precisely to give up my finite understanding and with it the power of discrimination that is natural to me, so that I may be able with divine madness to give thanks always' (ibid.: 156). While historical knowledge (which is speculative-dialectically attained by the concept's potentiality that is immanent in it) encloses the element of singularity within the anonymous order of a tyrannical totality, the decision of faith interrupts the closure of immanence and wrests the singular individual free from totality:

> Looked at world-historically, one ethically true principle, and the vital force in the ethical, becomes untrue: the relationship of possibility that everyone has towards God . . . thus, in the world-historical process as human beings see it, God does not play the rule of the Lord. Just as the ethical fails to appear in the process, so too one does not see God there . . . in the world-historical process the dead are not called to life, but only to an imaginary objective life and God in a fantastic sense the soul in progress. In the world-historical process God is tight-laced into a half-metaphysical, half-aesthetic-dogmatic bodice of property, which is immanence, the devil of a way to be God. (Ibid.: 131)

This is already an anticipation of Rosenzweigian-Lévinasian messianic affirmation of singularity outside the violence of totality. As with Rosenzweig and Lévinas, what affirms the singularity – which always *diachronically* sets itself apart from the universal – is the ethico-religious: the world-historical totalising process of politics does not know the ethical and the religious. It is this absence of the ethico-religious that gives the 'dizzying dialectic' the false sense of infinity; it thereby masks the evil and tyranny of totality in the name of a world-historical progress:

> that the ethical is in world history, as it is everywhere where God is, is not on that account denied, but only that the finite spirit can truly see it there, and to try to see it there is a piece of presumptuous risk-taking that can easily end with the observer losing the ethical to himself. (Ibid.: 118)

The ethico-religious, whose essence for Kierkegaard is eschatological, is the true 'breath of the eternal' (ibid.: 126): by precisely absolving the singulars from the tyranny of the anonymous order of totality, it reconciles 'fellowship with every human being' (ibid.: 127). The affirmation of singularity which Kierkegaard often calls 'the individual' or 'the particular' or 'the subjective', is not the narcissistic-virile self-assertion of a self-interested individual; it is precisely a more originary thinking of a genuine and generous fellowship in community, an eschatological community, not the community where the particulars are violently subjugated by the force of the law, but that community of the persecuted who have abandoned the violence of the law in the name of a divine love which is a madness and foolishness for the world.

> Yes, it is indeed madness. It is always madness to venture, but to risk everything for the expectation of an eternal happiness is total madness . . . if I am totally to venture, and totally strive for the highest good, there must be uncertainty, and I must, if I may put it in this way, have room to move. But the largest space I can move in, where there is room enough for the most intense gesture of the passion of the infinite, is uncertainty of knowledge regarding an eternal happiness, or the fact that the choice is in a finite sense madness; there, now there is room, now you can venture. (Ibid.: 357–8)

What, then, affirms and is affirmed unconditionally, outside totality, is indeed madness. Without the trial and the peril of the impossible – 'to be joyful out on the 70,000 fathoms deep' (ibid.: 117) – there is no ethics, and no ethical responsibility. But to be ethically responsible we need a measure which must exceed all measures, the measure which must, thus, be the immeasurable par excellence: one can't participate in this immeasurable measure without at once staking one's very existence in peril, without having to traverse through all possible travail – the very travail of existence – and without being exposed to the trial of the impossible: 'the trial is the religious paradigm's highest earnestness' (ibid.: 221). For Climacus – and for Kierkegaard – faith is the peril through which the immeasurable arrives in existence. Thus,

> Sitting calmly in a ship in fair weather is no image of faith; but when the ship has sprung a leak, enthusiastically to keep it afloat by manning the pumps yet not seeking harbour: that is the image. And if, in the long run, the image contains the impossibility, then this is an imperfection only in the image, but faith holds out. While the understanding, like the despairing passenger, stretches its arms out towards the sphere, faith works for the dear life in the depths: joyful and triumphant it saves the soul against the understanding. Existing in faith is that kind of contradiction . . . seeing that an eternal spirit exists is itself a contradiction. (Ibid.: 189, footnote)

This faith is said to have two tasks: 'first to look out for and at every instant discover the improbability, the paradox, so as then to keep hold of it with the passion of inwardness' (ibid.: 195). This paradox ('to be joyful out on the 70,000 fathoms deep') of faith is the true image of infinity, while the infinity of 'the dizzying dialectic' is only an endless and immanent mirror reproduction of the identical that immediately looks for the harbour, for it cannot work at the depth of existence (which is an abyss). The true eternal is not reached by the despairing passenger but 'which has been won through death' (ibid.: 198). Only s/he who has suffered the 'collision of finite and infinite' (ibid.: 195), without mediating it via a sublating concept, knows how to work at the depth of 70,000 fathoms. As against the false infinity and the false universality of the mediating concept, Kierkegaard evokes the *paradox* as the eschatological image of infinity when dialectic comes to a standstill. For each subjective thinker, existence is this standing still of dialectic – in wonder – when there is a pause, a halt and a sudden coincidence of the incommensurable: that the immeasurable has broken through the order of finitude!

The *historicality* of this breakthrough is more originally historical than the world-historical process: the *historicality* of faith is to be distinguished, by intensification of the paradox, from the Hegelian theodicy of history. The eschatological character of this originary *historicality* can be distinguished by its an-economy of faith, and by its radical diachrony: 'even the highest price is no merit, since the highest price is precisely to be willing to do everything yet knowing that this is nothing, and still to will it' (ibid.: 194). The extremity of diachrony is martyrdom, 'that martyrdom of believing against the understanding, the deadly peril of lying upon the 70,000 fathoms, only there to find God' (ibid.: 195), for 'to believe against the understanding that is martyrdom' (ibid.: 196). This *historicality* of faith where the profane history is disjoined from its very foundation: this disjointure is the *very event of history* which is experienced as martyrdom. What through Climacus Kierkegaard is interested in is not so much what takes places in (world) history but *the very event of history* when history itself takes place at the moment of degree zero. What takes place at the moment of degree zero is the absolute paradox, when the paradox itself is paradoxical. It is this event of history when the eternal happens in time by disrupting the continuum of all self-presence. It is this event of history that Hegel's 'dizzying dialectic' cannot think. To think this unthinkable is the peril of thought and is the vertigo of the concept: here the speculative concept falters, unable to make any more movement than the conceptual movement, while the sublime event of history, out of the abyss of freedom, demands not a conceptual movement but the eternal decision of faith. This is because it is the decision of faith that alone freely leaps over and transcends the totality of knowledge. Therefore, Kierkegaard calls faith 'passion' that, each time, transcends the totality of historical knowledge:

> But the highest power of every passion is always to will its own annihilation. Thus it is also the highest passion of understanding to desire an obstacle, despite the fact that the obstacle in one way or another may be its downfall. This is the highest paradox of thought, to want to discover something it cannot think. This passion of thought is fundamentally present everywhere in thought, also in the thought of the individual, to the extent that in thinking he transcends himself. (Kierkegaard 2009a: 111)

But it is this transcendence of faith that Hegel's speculative-secular theodicy does not know. Instead, Hegel takes away the apocalyptic sting of this transcendence, neutralises it and subsumes it within the immanent order of speculative-hypothetic 'unity of thought and being'. The result of this secularised eschatology is everywhere to be seen: the apotheosis or deification of the world-historical process as it exists, and the apology for the triumphal march of the theodicy that ends up in the justification of the evil in the name of a pre-determinate *telos*.

Therefore, the Kierkegaardian concept of existence – existence that holds itself out towards the abyss of faith in decision – has to be understood in light of the eschatological suffering which the Son of God himself undergoes on the cross. This abyssal moment of suffering cannot be a mere transitional instance, as one instance among others, within the homogeneous scale of an empty, linear world-historical time: it is the very inauguration or event of history which is also a break as much as a qualitative leap. 'To believe [this] against understanding', 'this faith's martyrdom' is madness (for it refuses to participate in the triumphal cry of world-historical Reason, and it voluntarily accepts suffering): it introduces an abyss right at the heart of the world, a pair of empty sockets that the eyes of Christ has become on the cross. Understood in that sense, to become Christian – which, each time, is a 'to become' – is to introduce the event of *kenosis* right at the heart of one's own singular and individual existence: emptying out the attributes of worldly power and abandoning, by a step back, the triumphal cries of world-historical politics; it is to introduce the *diachrony* of contemporaneity at the heart of synchronic world-order (of worldly sovereignty) by the cision of an eternal de-cision.

It is by virtue of this surprise of the *eschaton* which is *to come* – un-programmable, incalculable and in excess of the economy of knowledge – that our existence is ecstatic, and is held open to the event of eternity in time. Because the Hegelian immanent theodicy of history includes the event of *eschaton* as an intra-mundane occurrence at the end of the world-historical process, it lacks that decisive element of surprise that comes from the future. Since the possibility of ethics is the very possibility of the eschatological future, Hegel's immanent theodicy of history lacks the decisive element of the ethical which alone can salvage existence from the empty infinity of 'the dizzying dialectic'.

> The Hegelian philosophy has no ethics, it has therefore never dealt with the future, which is essentially the element or medium of ethics. The Hegelian philosophy contemplates the past, the six thousand years of world-history, and then is busy in pointing out every particular development as a transitory factor in the world-historical process. (Kierkegaard 1994: 262)

'Ethics therefore looks with a distrustful eye on all world-historical knowledge' (Kierkegaard 2009b: 111). The world-historical knowledge aesthetically neutralises 'the absolute ethical distinction between good and evil' (ibid.), a distinction which is essentially the qualitative distinction, irreducible to the quantitative order of the world-historical knowledge. It is precisely because Hegelian theodicy lacks 'the ethics of futurity' that it can't think the fundamental existential character of existence: that existence as, each time, *to come*; its passionate intensity that restlessly ventures ahead; its transcendence that does not shy away from the sting of death. This Kierkegaardian understanding of existence, as I have mentioned above, is very much Schellingian in inspiration: that is, it is not enough to make the category of existence mobile; one must wrest the event of existence from the categorical grasp of the concept, and render it a 'becoming' without participating in the dialectical 'movement' of speculation, in 'the hypothetical unity of thought and being'; it is not enough to have a logical category called 'Reality', one has to bring existentially the de-cision that arrests the logical mobility of the system, and inaugurate another 'becoming':

> Someone existing is constantly coming to be; the genuinely existing subjective thinker stimulates this existence of his constantly in his thinking and invests all his thinking in becoming. It is the same as with style: the only

writer who really has style is the one who never has anything finished, but 'troubles the waters of language'(John 5: 4) every time he begins, so that for him the most everyday expression comes into being with the pristine freshness of a new birth. (Ibid.: 73)

To think of this 'pristine freshness of a new birth', the quantitative determination of temporality has to be de-formalised. Only existence as spirit – and not as concept – is an infinite striving (understood subjectively). This *infinitisation*, without it being teleologically determined, is at once an intensification and acceleration. Qualitatively understood, the eschatological intensity of the moment is that where 'every delay means mortal danger and the decision is so infinitely important as to be so instantly urgent as to make the opportunity appears to have gone by ungrasped' (ibid.: 169). Such intensification of the qualitative disjunction – for the qualitative is by definition disjunctive – is both pathetic and comic. The Hegelian equalisation of infinity with the universality of the concept denies this tragic disparate of the spirit that leads him (Hegel) to give up the singularity of subjective existence and take his consolation in the world-historical objectivity: 'From the point of view of pathos, a single second has infinite value; viewed comically, 10,000 years are but a foolish trick, just like yesterday, and yet the time in which the existing individual lives consists of just such parts' (ibid.: 78). Pathos and comic are, thus, two modes of de-formalisation of the quantitative determination of time. Again,

> In relation to an eternal truth that is to decide my eternal happiness, eighteen centuries have no greater demonstrative force than a single day. On the contrary, the eighteen centuries and all, yes all these countless things that can be told and said and repeated in that connection, have a power to divert which distracts excellently. (Ibid.: 41)

Pathos and comic are two modes of de-formalisation of the quantitative, homogeneous determination of time because 'at the root' of them

> lies the disparity, the contradiction, between the infinite and the finite, the eternal and the becoming . . . the disparity grasped in view of the idea ahead is pathos; grasped with the idea behind, it is comedy. When the subjective existing thinker turns his face towards the idea, the grasping of this discrepancy is in pathos; when he turns his back to the idea and lets it cast its rays from behind into the same disparity, the grasping of it is in comedy. (Ibid.: 76)

The intensification of this *disparate* leads to the paradox 'and Christianity is precisely the paradoxical' (ibid.: 89).

The spirituality of Christian existence – where existence itself is to be understood as 'spirit' – manifests this disparate as either/or. In the immanent sphere of aesthetic life, this either/or does not appear as an unconditional disjunction, while in the ethico-religious spheres the disjunction is absolute and unconditional: this means that the disparate *as* disparate, and not (conceptual) representation of the disparate, is the very condition of possibility of the manifestation of the ethico-religious. The absence of either/or is possible (or, the dialectical sublation of either/or is possible) only when thought is abstraction, and when existence is altogether abrogated. In the realm of existence, either/or is the impasse of thought, and is the extreme limit of the thinkable:

> It is only where everything is in the course of becoming, where only so much eternity is present as can keep hold of the passionate decision, where eternity relates as the future to the one who is on the way to being – it is there that the absolute disjunction belongs. When I put together eternity and becoming, it is not repose that I get but the future. That, no doubt, is why Christianity has proclaimed Christianity as the future, preached, as it was, in existence, for which reason it also assumes an absolute aut/aut. (Ibid.: 257)

The 'dizzying dialectic' of the Hegelian system lacks the element of the ethical because he understands the existing individual only as belonging to a generation, and because he understands himself only on the basis of this finality: ' he can understand only what is past and done with' (ibid.). In a more degrading manner than the Socratic (who was indeed a bit *Atopos*) recollection, the pagan mythical mode of understanding phenomenon on the basis of 'the hypothetical unity of thought and being' swallows up the ethics of futurity. The singular element of the ethical – the intensification of the 'each one' – is irreducible to the number: the singular remains, thus, the unaccountable remnant, a 'not taking one in ten' (ibid.: 268), an outside of totality. In this sense, singularity which is 'each time', *hic et nunc*, the singularity to come, is the true image of infinity; it is the true image of the ethico-religious by virtue of the manifestation of the absolute disparate in it as the disparate without any dialectical-speculative mediation. Kierkegaard calls this singularity to come of existence as 'spirit'. In this Kierkegaard sense, Hegel's phenomenology of spirit cannot be called the true phenomenology of spirit, if phenomenology is to be understood as the phenomenalisation of spirit, which is the manifestation of the absolute disjunction. The true phenomenology is the phenomenology that tears apart 'the hypothetical unity of thought and being' by introducing the decision of faith out of the abyss of freedom.

If the subsumption of the singulars under the power of the universal constitutes the tyranny of totality, only infinitisation – 'to come' – of the singulars can introduce the element of the ethical: 'the desperate attempt of the abortive Hegelian ethics to make the state the highest ethical authority is a most unethical attempt to finitize individuals, or unethical flight from the category of the individual into that of race' (ibid.: 422, footnote). Only 'the paradoxical accentuation of existence' (ibid.: 482) makes available the empty measure of space where the spirit is nailed to the cross, where understanding is crucified, and spirit 'with divine madness gives thanks'. Spirit – nailed to the cross and crucified – is, then, truly the religious existence: it is this religiosity, eschatologically understood, that decisively breaks away from the anonymous world-order of the secular-historical Reason. It is this theologico-political gesture that makes Kierkegaard spiritually akin to Schelling's Christian and Rosenzweig's Jewish messianic interruption: the whole question is Christianity's (without Christendom) *break* from the order of worldly *potestas*, the break that takes its point of departure from the fundamental experience of human suffering and death, and that eschatologically-messianically opens itself to redemption *to come*.

Idolatry and omnipresence

The radical break or the qualitative disjunction that paradoxically accentuates existence – existence that each time is singular – demands a qualitative dialectic of becoming (which is not 'movement'): the expression of this qualitative dialectic is not the transparency and intelligibility of direct communication, but a breach into the immanent plane of the universal communicability. As there is no such thing called 'death in general' – for death is each time singular – so, existential communication, which affirms 'singularity to come' (Schürmann) outside the order of totality, can only be 'indirect communication': 'the highest principle of all thought can be demonstrated only indirectly (negatively)' (ibid.: 185).

> If the task is to become subjective, then thinking death is not at all something in general, but indeed an action, for the development of the subjectivity consists precisely in his actively implicating himself in his thought about his own existence. (Ibid.: 142)

The thought of death is, thus, intimately interwoven with the problem of communication: this thought of death consists of giving up or renouncing all 'finite understanding' and abandoning all the powers that govern us in our natural life. This mortification of the worldly order of sovereign powers is a dark night where speech too, in its intricate connection with death, undergoes destitution. Therefore, Franz Rosenzweig too, following Kierkegaard, begins his deconstruction of the hegemonic ontology from 'Ionia to Jena' with his thought of death.[2] Because the singular experience of the subjective thinker refuses the mediation of the concept, the communication of it can only be a 'negative communication', and the theological politics that puts into question the hegemonic order of the law can only be a 'negative' theological politics. It is not directly political communication because the ethico-religious exceeds the sphere of the political; but, indirectly, this religious transcendence over the political has immense political significance. Both Kierkegaard's *kenotic* eschatology and Rosenzweig's messianic 'religion' affirm this transcendence of the 'theological' ('eschatological' and 'messianic') over (world-historical) politics. This *transcendence* is not neutralisation of the political as in secular-liberal thought; and yet, at the same time, it is not merely 'politics' in the bare sense of the term.

For both Kierkegaard and Rosenzweig the thought of death is, thus, not (directly) a political question: it is a profoundly religious experience par excellence, for it is the sphere of the religious that decisively affirms the singularity of the individual over and against the total order of significations. If the order of the totality of signification (and, thus, of universal communication) is a 'work of death' – as Hegel famously says[3] – then the singular encounter with one's death can only have an indirect communication. Here, death refuses the work of the concept that culminates in the general order of universal communication. The dialectic that only negatively communicates – thus indicatively and not predicatively – this truth of the way[4] is the dialectic of 'the non-identical' that refuses the violent law of subsumption (see Adorno 1981). In the universal order of the law that has abrogated existence and annulled the element of singularity, particular beings are grasped (*greifen*) by the concept (*Begriff*) as dead beings: this is why law appears as the work of death. In the total order of the law, beings always already appear as dead: it is the dead people the universal order of the law demands. This is why Kierkegaard can rightly say, contra Hegel, that 'in the world-historical process the dead are not called to life, but only to an imaginary objective life' (Kierkegaard 2009b: 131). On the other hand, the whole intensity of religious existence is concentrated in this impossible hope for resurrection, that the dead will be called to life again. Only then can the mythic violence of the profane order expire totally without having to return it again; only then is the vicious circle of violence suspended, and redemption becomes a certainty, not an objective certainty but a certainty in faith.

This impossible hope, this hope against hope (Paul 4: 18) that the dead may come alive again, this apocalyptic hope that everything can be made anew, and that death is not the final event of existence, and that there is still a time to come: this eschatological affirmation cannot be embodied in the world-historical process of universal movement. It can only be indirectly communicated. All direct communication of this truth loses its 'way', because the truth is the truth of the way. Taking away this apocalyptic way-character of truth, all direct communication ends up in pantheism and paganism. Since existence, which is each time singular, refuses the finality of the system, and the finality of direct communication, existence is 'an absolute protest against the system':

> every system must be pantheistic just because of its finality. Existing must be annulled in the eternal before the system can bring itself to a close; there must be no existing remainder . . . [existence] is an absolute protest against the system. (Kierkegaard 2009b: 104)

Thus, by taking away the apocalyptic sting of the paradoxical intensification of the disjunction, Hegelian theodicy has ended up in the 'speculative confusion of the ethical with the world-historical'. In that sense, Hegelian theodicy of history is a kind of paganism and a pantheistic system, for,

> All paganism consists in this, that God relates to man directly, as the striking to the struck. But the spiritual relationship to God by the breakthrough of inwardness that corresponds to the divine artfulness that God has nothing, absolutely nothing about him that is striking. (Ibid.: 205)

Hegel's theodicy may have constituted itself speculatively on the dialectical modal of the cross, but, peculiarly, his theology of the Good Friday knows not the mystery of suffering which lies in the *kenotic* manifestation of Christ. This speculative-theological investment of Hegel on the Good Friday that peculiarly takes away (as if it were possible!) the *kenotic* disfigurement of Christ on the cross, has ended up in idolatry of a sort: 'in paganism the direct relation is idolatry' (ibid.: 206). The conceptual mediation of the Hegelian dialectic could not transform the idolatry of direct communication into the existential dialectic of indirect communication because it cannot mediate this absolute paradox which faith alone can affirm: that the omnipresence of God can only be invisibility. It is this incomprehensible paradox which interrupts the idolatry of any possible direct relationship between God and man: the 'relation between omnipresence and invisibility is like that between secrecy and revelation' (ibid.: 206):

> Nature, the totality of creation, is God's work. And yet God is not there but within the individual human being there is a possibility (according to his possibility he is spirit) that is awakened in inwardness into a God-relationship, and then it is possible to see God everywhere. (Ibid.: 206–7)

This 'inwardness of truth' is 'the separation with which each for himself is existing in what is true' (ibid.: 208). This inwardness is an 'indirect polemic against speculation' (ibid.: 211). This irreducible and absolute separation refuses the theologico-political principle of *analogia entis*: 'there is no analogy to the sphere of the paradox religions' (ibid.: 475). 'The qualitative dialectic of the spheres' that passes through and endures 'the crucifixion of the understanding' (ibid.: 472) is precisely 'the breach with immanence' (ibid.: 479) that makes any direct recognisability impossible for the creaturely being. 'God's essential invisibility' (ibid.: 487) limits the theologico-political principle of *analogia entis*, for this essential invisibility calls forth not analogy but paradox. While the paradox by virtue of its indirect communication *indicates* existence as actuality, analogy understands the order of being as poetic-mythic; while paradox is the religious communication par excellence, analogy is the expression of the form of life in its aesthetic-immanent sphere. Therefore, and this is absolutely important,

> Christianity is the absolute paradox precisely because it destroys a possibility (the analogy of paganism, an eternal god-becoming) as an illusion and turns it into actuality and just this is the paradox. (Ibid.: 488)

This is the paradox: the hope for unconditional and eternal happiness 'makes suffering the mark of the Christian's happiness' (ibid.: 489). This absolute paradox knows no analogy; even the suffering of Christ knows no analogy to the suffering of martyrs, believers or heroes of intellect. 'The martyrs' destiny, when they came into the world, was not to suffer; their destiny was one thing and the other, and it was to accomplish it that they had to suffer, endure suffering, face death; but the suffering is not the *telos*'. But the absolute paradox of Christ is that 'Christ entered the world in order to suffer'. 'Indeed, what distinguishes the absolute paradox is that every analogy is a fraud' (ibid.: 503). Here is Kierkegaard's decisive eschatological deconstruction of the theologico-political principle of *analogia entis*: God, in his invisibility, belongs neither to the order of being nor to the order of relation. Paradox is the relation to the wholly other without relation!

The paradox of Christ is not that God has become (the race called) man but rather that God has become an absolutely singular and irreducible individual whose singularity is, nevertheless, unrecognisable: such is God's *kenosis* that the event of revelation refuses to be communicated directly. Precisely because this event is the event of existence – an actual existence, and as such is singular, and not a hypothetical possibility – it remains unthinkable and incognito; it refuses the idolatry of direct representation. Thus, unrecognisability is not mere negation of revelation: this 'negativity' belongs to the very affirmative advent of pure revelation, because it is not a revelation of a specific object of cognition in the world but an affirmation of pure *announcing* of itself which, nevertheless, remains irreducible to all cognitive categories and predications. Revelation is the pure event of proclamation. What idolatry is on one hand, chatter is on the other: the reduction of the singularity of the event of revelation into an intra-mundane occurrence in the world-historical process; the reduction of the 'actuality without potentiality' (in Schelling's terms) into endless, virtual circulation of mere possibility, into the hypothetical 'idea-existence' (ibid.: 277):

> The object of faith is therefore the god's actuality in the sense of existence. But to exist means first and foremost to be the particular individual, and this is why thought must disregard existence, for the particular cannot be thought, only the universal. The object of faith is therefore the actuality of god in existence, i.e., as a particular individual, i.e., that the god has actually been there as an individual human being. (Ibid.: 273)

These words could well have been written by Schelling too, or by Rosenzweig. This whole gesture consists of releasing the event of revelation (therefore, the existence sphere of the religious) from the immanent metaphysics of pantheism. Like Schelling, and also like Heidegger, Kierkegaard is the great thinker of beginning. The actual beginning of existence, and not the logical beginning of the system, does not happen with the general assertion of the 'pure being' which, being devoid of any particularity, is equal to 'pure nothing'. The actual beginning of existence is the act of decision that brings to a halt the whole procession of reflection and brings this process to an end. The actual, not the hypothetical, beginning always begins with the singular: thus, it cannot begin without presupposition.

> To require a decision is to abandon the presuppositionlessness. It is only when reflection comes to a halt that a beginning can be made, and reflection can be halted only by something else, and this something else is something quite other than the logical, because it is a decision. And only when the beginning that brings the process of reflection to a halt is a breakthrough, so that the absolute beginning itself breaks through the infinitely continued reflection, only then is it that the beginning has no presuppositions. If, on the other hand, it is a break in which the process of reflection is interrupted, so that the beginning can emerge, then the beginning is not the absolute, since it has come about through a shift to another genus. (Ibid.: 96)

This means nothing other than the following: the system is impossible to begin with! The Hegelian system cannot make any genuine beginning because any beginning, 'when *made*, does not occur on the strength of immanent thinking but is *made* on the strength of a decision, essentially on the strength of faith' (ibid.: 159). But the singular is unthinkable. This is why Schelling could write – and here too Kierkegaard follows him closely – that the beginning of thought is the unthought: the unthought or the un-pre-thinkable (*Unvordenkliche*) exuberance of existence is precisely the beginning of thought. What is that absolutely unthought if not this absolute paradox, which is (not that God has become man, but) that God has become a single individual?

> The absurd is that the eternal truth has come about in time, that God has come about, has been born, has grown up, etc., has come about just as the single human being, indistinguishable from any other, since all immediate recognisability is pre-Socratic paganism and from the Jewish point of view idolatry. (Ibid.: 177)

It is the absurd that is the object of faith and the only thing that permits of faith' (ibid.). But this faith is the peril of thinking and the crucifixion of understanding. If the beginning is to be made, it is this shipwreck of existence that precisely must be affirmed, which faith alone can do: 'without risk, no faith. Faith is just this, the contradiction between the infinite passion of inwardness and objective uncertainty' (ibid.: 171–2). Faith is that 'something else', that absolutely heterogeneous other that transcendently breaks through the closure of immanence and tears it apart. 'The incommensurability between a historical truth and an eternal decision' (ibid.: 83) interrupts the immanent continuum of the pantheistic system and disrupts the idolatry of representation. What cannot be represented and recognised, within the totality of signification, is this very decisive beginning itself where lies an absolute paradox: 'the paradox emerges when the eternal truth and existence are put together; but every time existence is marked out, the paradox becomes ever clearer' (ibid.: 175).[5]

What the historicality of Christianity introduces with the absolute paradox of faith, then, is the *spacing* of freedom from the closure of 'mythic commensurability' (ibid.: 504). The mythic 'commensurability is direct recognisability'; on the other hand, 'the form of the servant is the incognito' (ibid.: 505). The *kenotic* form of the God, in his unrecognisability, suspends the law of 'the mythic commensurability' of the worldly order. This *kenotic* nihilation of the mythic order of immanence can only be indirectly – negatively – communicated: it is the secret par excellence, an absolute and irreducible secret. The incommensurability of the paradox cannot be bridged by any analogy, and that is why it is difficult or, rather, impossible, to become a Christian, for to become a Christian is to be 'nailed to the paradox of having based eternal happiness on the relation to something historical'. The paradox is thus the cross. The immanent metaphysics of Hegelian pantheism has transformed this cross 'speculatively into an eternal history, the god-in-time into an eternal god-becoming, etc.'(ibid.: 485): the result is the deification of the worldly order as it already exists, and an apology for the worldly sovereignty on a supposedly theological foundation. As against this immanent order of 'mythic commensurability' which is Hegel's theodicy, Kierkegaard invokes the 'paradoxical-dialectical' where 'every remainder of original immanence [is] annihilated, and all connection [is] severed . . . then we have the *paradox-religious*'. This paradox-religious arrives only at the place when 'the individual [is] placed at the very edge of existence', when existence itself becomes as if crucified (ibid.: 479). The singular existing individual has to kenotically empty all commensuration of immanence to have the paradox-religiosity of the Christian faith.

In the mythic order of immanence where the logic of commensuration rules, guilt appears as something external, and punishment strikes as force (which is part of natural justice). In this manner, as it is portrayed in the mythic-tragic play, the possible commensuration between guilt and punishment is the very law of retributive justice. In this order 'immediacy expires in misfortune' (ibid.: 366). In the religious order of the existence sphere, on the other hand, guilt is not experienced as external and as misfortune: the guilt consciousness of the sinner in the religious sphere is, thus, irreducible to the aesthetic-metaphysical order of *nemesis*. This guilt consciousness of the religious sinner cannot be atoned in the retributive justice that operates on the logic of commensuration between guilt and punishment. It needs an unconditional grace that must be gratuitously given beyond the economy of retributive justice. This means that the justice of grace unconditionally exceeds the retributive justice of the immanent order: by suspending the operation of work and law, grace breaks through immanence and resurrects the dead unto new life. While in the immanent order of 'mythic commensurability' retributive justice strikes the guilty with the force of fate, grace infinitely exceeds fate, and infinitely exceeds the judgement of the law: 'This is the Gospel, the glad tidings, that the cruelty of fate is abolished' (Kierkegaard 1994: 224).

While misfortune strikes us in the mythic order of commensuration, in the religious sphere the paradox appears as martyrdom that eschatologically redeems us from death. Therefore, the religious suffering should be distinguished from the misfortune of immediate life. While misfortunate strikes us with the mythic-tragic violence of the law, religious suffering is the point of departure towards absolute freedom in God: 'the religious address claims for itself the respectful freedom to take being human along quite directly, pretty much like death, which also takes human beings along directly' (Kierkegaard 2009b: 368). Therefore, 'suffering belongs to the religious life essentially' (ibid.: 371); it is a 'form of the highest life' (ibid.: 372).[6] The suffering consists of being 'nothing at all before God, or to be nothing at all and be thereby before God' (ibid.: 387): the worldly attributes of the aesthetic-immanent form of life (where sovereignty rules supreme on the basis of power) enter here destitution and impoverishment. This suffering also consists of undergoing the offence of the paradox: 'the paradox, which requires faith against the understanding, brings out the offense straight away, whether more closely defined as the offense that suffers or as the offense that mocks the paradox as foolishness' (ibid.: 492). When one takes away the offensive character of the cross, Christianity becomes idolatry. This is, then, decisively the Christian existential pathos: redemption through suffering, or happiness through martyrdom. Because the divine glory cannot be directly recognised on the profane and unredeemed order, the indirect communication of the indicative ethico-religious pathos has to essentially bear the secret:

> The ordinary communication, objective thinking, has no secrets; it is only with doubly reflected subjective thinking that secrets arise, i.e. all of its essential content is essentially secrecy because it cannot be imparted directly. This is the meaning of secrecy. The fact that the knowledge in question is not to be said directly, because the essential thing with the knowledge is the appropriation, makes it a secret for everyone who is not in the same way doubly reflected within himself. (Ibid.: 67)[7]

Suffering here is the suffering of the secret, and hence is the mystery par excellence, the paschal mystery! For the world to be redeemed, it has to undergo the paschal mystery of suffering on the cross.

The secret of responsibility

The secret, for Kierkegaard, essentially belongs to the religious sphere of existence. In the immanent order of the aesthetic life, the secret is accidental. The essential secret is the offence to the light of the law: the law seeks to abrogate the secret of the religious existence of the singular, subjective thinker, and subsumes it to the anonymous order of totality. The essential secret is not the private, interior secret of the isolated, private individual against the public, general order of intelligibility; the essential secret refuses the interiorising act of the dialectical-speculative memory: the concept cannot trace the secret back to a particular subjectivity and sublate it to the universal order of intelligibility. In that sense, the secret is the immemorial event of existence par excellence; and it is the infinite responsibility of the subjective thinker to maintain the secret as secret, as if it is impossible to be responsible without being-secret.

In his *Fear and Trembling*, Kierkegaard-Johannes de Silentio brings the very idea of an infinite responsibility (the absolute relation to the absolute) out of the trial of the impossible: the absolute responsibility to the absolute demands from Abraham the absolute sacrifice, the unconditional renunciation of all worldly power and human potency, of human wisdom and worldly calculability of knowledge, of all *oikonomia* of debt and return, and of the very possibility of human communication. In Abraham's sacrifice of his beloved son Isaac (which without this an-economy of the impossible is a murder in the eyes of the world), it is not the law and labour of the concept but the very logic of *kenosis* that is at work. The *kenosis* is the absolute paradox:

> There was one who was great by reason of his power, and one who was great by reason of his wisdom, and one who was great by reason of his hope, and one who was great by reason of his love; but Abraham was greater than all, great by reason of his power whose strength is impotence, great by reason of his wisdom whose secret is foolishness, great by reason of his hope whose form is madness, great by reason of his love which is hatred of oneself. (Kierkegaard 1994: 12)

That Abraham is great by reason of his impotency, of his foolishness, of his madness and of his hatred of oneself: this is not the truth of the world; this does not take the form of the world. Only by de-forming the form of the world and dis-figuring the figure of the 'human' subject can the truth be grasped as truth: the paradox hanging on the cross. This cross of understanding refuses any worldly mediation, for all worldly mediation demands the universal, while this suffering of the paradox is absolutely singular relation to the absolutely singular. This is the paradox because here 'the individual is higher than the universal' and is even superior, 'that it is the particular individual who, after he has been subordinated as the particular to the universal' rises above the universal and thus stands 'in an absolute relation to the absolute. This position cannot be mediated, for all mediation comes about precisely by virtue of the universal, inaccessible to thought' (ibid.: 46–7). Therefore, paradox is something inhospitable, a scandal and an offence to the world, it is something incommunicable in the language of the world. That is why Abraham 'speaks no human language. Though he himself understood all the tongues of the world, though his loved ones also understood them, he nevertheless cannot speak – he speaks a divine language . . . he "speaks with tongues"' (ibid.: 101–2). The sub-text here is *The Acts of the Apostles*: 'And there appeared unto them cloven tongues like as of fire, and it sat upon each of them. And they were all filled with the Holy Ghost, and began to speak with other tongues, as the Spirit gave them utterance' (Acts 2: 3–4). Here is the eloquence of the apostles who speak with divine tongues gifted to them by the Holy Ghost, while Abraham is the silent one, in secret, in absolute relation to the absolute, as the singular individual outside the ethical order of the universal, alone and incommunicable.

The absolute responsibility that Abraham maintains in his absolute secrecy and in absolute fidelity is, paradoxically, also the highest irresponsibility, seen from the ethical point of view: Kierkegaard-de Silentio never forgets to remind us again and again of the murderous character of Abraham's act. The irresponsibility lies in Abraham keeping himself in secret: the universal, anonymous order of the ethical is the order of absolute disclosure which cannot tolerate the secrecy of the singular that refuses the dazzling intelligibility of the ethical. There is, then, a violence of the ethical, a metaphysical *arché-violence*: the reduction of all secrecy and, thus, responsibility itself to the intelligibility of the universal light.

Kierkegaard-de Silentio, however, makes a distinction between the silence of the aesthetic and the secrecy of the religious paradox: the aesthetic can speak but keeps silent, while Abraham cannot speak and therefore keeps silent. The last words of Abraham (with which he replies to Isaac: 'God will provide Himself the lamb for the burnt offering, my son'), then, can neither be understood as the silence of the aesthetic hero nor be understood as the speech of the ethical-universal order: as a form of irony, rigorously speaking, this saying of Abraham does not renounce secrecy to the order of universal intelligibility (as does the tragic hero), and at the same time it is not the mere muteness of the aesthetic sphere of life. 'Here again it appears that one may have an understanding of Abraham, but [it] can understand him only in the same way as one understands the paradox' (Kierkegaard 1994: 106). This incomprehensible paradox exceeds both the silence of the aesthetic sphere of life and the universal intelligibility of the ethical sphere. The secrecy of the paradox rather *spaces* existence open to the wholly other, in unconditional responsibility with the risk – without which there is no responsibility – that it may appear in the order of constituted phenomenality precisely as an absolute irresponsibility. This makes the suffering of the knight of faith even more abysmal than the suffering of the tragic hero: the tragic hero renounces the immediate enjoyment of the aesthetic sphere of life for the sake of, or *in sight of*, the universal order of totality. Here, the immediate enjoyment of the aesthetic sphere of life is indeed lost, but this movement of resignation still finds consolation in the life of the universal intelligibility: in this, renunciation or resignation of calculation and economy of exchange does not yet reach the absolute paradox, which Kierkegaard calls 'the teleological suspension of the ethical':

> The difference between the tragic hero and Abraham is clearly evident. The tragic hero still remains within the ethical. He lets the expression of the ethical find its *telos* in a higher expression of the ethical; the ethical relation between father and son, or daughter and father, he reduces to a sentiment which has its dialectic in its relation to the idea of morality. Here there can be no question of a teleological suspension of the ethical. (Ibid.: 49–50)

In the renunciation of the tragic hero – Agamemnon sacrificing Iphigenia – the mythic violence of the law is still not suspended but is reinforced: Kierkegaard here displaces the mythic-tragic order of suffering in the profane order and opens it to a still more paradoxical suffering of the religious existence. The latter, bereft of all consolation and refusal of all ethical intelligibility, is truly the exception in regard to the law which does not restitute the law in turn; what, rather, it restitutes is the originary incommensuration, always singular in eschatological sense, which is always higher than the lucidity of the universal:

> Thus, for example, if we suppose that the church requires such a sacrifice of one of its members, we have in this case only a tragic hero. For the idea of the church is not qualitatively different from that of the state, insofar as the individual comes into the paradox he does not reach the idea of the church; he does not come out of the paradox, but in it he must find either his blessedness or his perdition. Such an ecclesiastical hero expressed in his act the universal, and there will be no one in the church – not even his father and mother, etc – who fails to understand him. (Ibid.: 64)

The theologico-political implication of this argument is unmistakable: the Church is not qualitatively opposed to the state, because both – as complementary orders of the universal – require 'revelation' and take offence against the absolute secrecy of the singular existence absolved from totality. The ecclesiastical hero and the tragic hero are complementary figures: the economy of the aesthetic enjoyment is sacrificed *in sight of* greater profit. This is why neither the tragic hero nor the ecclesiastical hero teleologically suspend the ethical: the loss returns, in a circular re-appropriation of the same, in surplus profit. On the other hand, the faith of Abraham implicates him in absolute sacrifice to the point of – as Jacques Derrida reminds us – sacrificing sacrifice: only this sacrifice affirms the absolute heterogeneity and an-economy of the wholly other, which for Kierkegaard-de Silentio is the wholly other God, *Dieu Absconditus*.

> In *in absconditio*, *absconditus* refers rather to the hidden, the secret, the mysterious as that which retreats into the invisible, that which is lost from sight. The majority of examples or figures on the basis of which *absconditus* has come to mean secrecy in general, and so has become synonymous with *secretum* (separate, retired, withdrawn from view), privilege the optical dimension. (Derrida 1992a: 89)

The absolute responsibility involves absolute loss or sacrifice – Abraham sacrificing Isaac – without return, of profit or gain, consolation or salvation. In this sense, Kierkegaard's faith must be rescued even from the economy of salvation, 'for when the individual by his guilt has gone outside the universal he can return to it only by virtue of having come as the individual into an absolute relationship with the absolute (Kierkegaard 1994: 86–7), which is no relationship. This secret is the absolute incommensurable, which is neither the concealment of the life of psyche nor the repose of the universal but the singularity of the *Pneuma*. Kierkegaard's pneumatic idea of faith is Pauline in spirit. In his *The Gift of Death* Jacques Derrida, however, does not relate Kierkegaard to Paul as much as to the Gospel of Matthew to underline the absolute an-economy and dissymmetry of Kierkegaardian faith. Thereby, Derrida rigorously dwells on this aporia of responsibility (that to be infinitely responsible is to be irresponsible) with which Kierkegaard-de Silentio, as much as the Gospel of Matthew, is concerned. Here is the one of the passages from Matthew that Derrida cites:

> Ye have heard that it hath been said, An eye for an eye, and a tooth for a tooth: But I say unto you, That ye resist not evil: but whosoever shall smite thee on thy right cheek, turn to him the other also. (5: 38–9)

In 'an eye for an eye, and a tooth for a tooth' there governs the logic of the law. What Christ teaches here is that which absolutely undoes, without profit in turn, the logic of symmetry and analogy. This heterogeneity between two hands and two cheeks is emphasised even more when Christ says: 'love your enemies, bless them that curse you, do good to them that hate you, and pray for them which despitefully use you, and persecute you' (5: 43–4). Derrida then evokes Carl Schmitt:

> It is more than ever necessary to quote the Latin or Greek, if only to remind us of the remark made by Carl Schmitt when, in chapter 3 of *The Concept of the Political* he emphasizes the fact that *inimicus* is not *hostis* in Latin and *ekhthros* is not *polemios* in Greek. This allows him to conclude that Christ's teaching concerns the love that we must show to our private enemies, those we would be tempted to hate through personal or subjective passion, and not to public enemies. (Derrida 1992a: 103)

Derrida shows that the essential secrecy which infinitely affirms absolute heterogeneity in the Gospel of Matthew is text that underlines Kierkegaard-de Silentio's secret of responsibility: the *Deus Absconditus* is the absolute secret whose invisibility or incognito forever eludes the grasp of manifestation. This dissymmetry, which is the dissymmetry of the gift of death, has immense theologico-political consequences for us: it undoes or unworks in advance the very symmetrical but oppositional logic of the Schmittean friend and enemy distinction. It is difficult, without terrible violence, both to the Gospel of Matthew and to the Kierkegaard-de Silentio text, to bring them under the possibility of Christian politics as Schmitt understands it. Derrida then goes on to cite the text from Leviticus:

> Thou shalt not hate thy brother in thine heart: thou shalt in any wise rebuke thy neighbour, and not suffer sin upon him.
>
> Thou shalt not avenge, nor bear any grudge against the children of thy people, but thou shalt love thy neighbour as thyself: I am the Lord. (Leviticus 19: 15–18)

'If one's neighbour is here one's *congener*', writes Derrida,

> someone from *my* community, from the same people or nation, then the person who can be opposed to him or her is the non-neighbour not as private enemy but as foreigners, as member of another nation, community or people. That runs counter to Schmitt's interpretation: the frontier between *inimicus* and *hostis* would be more permeable than he wants to believe. (Derrida 1992a: 105)

With the intensification of this eschatological difference which Kierkegaard calls either/or ('so either there is a paradox, that the individual as the individual stands in an absolute relation to the absolute/or Abraham is lost' (Kierkegaard 1994: 107)) the theological-analogical foundation of (Schmittean) politics is separated and is given over to the secrecy. Secrecy, then, for Kierkegaard, is eschatological event of separation: it introduces the irreducible and inhospitable fissure into the continuum of any direct communication. In other words, secrecy makes the idolatry of representation impossible. Abraham's communication with Isaac – his last enigmatic words – is such indirect communication: the universal intelligibility of being of the ethical order is surpassed and transcended without falling thereby into the aesthetic-mute suffering. With this eschatological suspension or surpassing of the tragic-mythic order of morality, and yet holding the disparate of life together (universal-singular), the order of totality – the very immanence of the world-historical politics – is kept open to what Kierkegaard calls 'the religious' whose essence is the eschatological suspension or surpassing of the legitimacy-seeking politics of the worldly order. While both Lévinas and Derrida think of this messianic surpassing of the conditioned order of political negotiation as the ethical openness to the infinite and irreducible Other, for Kierkegaard it is the eschatological opening of the violence of historical reason to the wholly Other of the God becoming a single, individual man and dying his most ignoble death on the cross. The paradox of the cross eschatologically puts into question the legitimacy of all world-historical *potestas* in the name of the unconditioned, the wholly other, *kenotic* love. In Abraham's secrecy the violence of the law of the concept – whose work is the work of mediation – is *kenotically* put into question, not in the name of another, albeit higher, hegemonic order of *potestas*, but in the name of the wholly other order of love that radically suspends all world-historical *potestas*.

Notes

1. 'To unite the moments of life in simultaneity, just that is the task' (Kierkegaard 2009b: 292).
2. 'For indeed, an All would not die and nothing would die in the All. Only the singular can die and everything mortal is solitary. Philosophy has to rid the world of what is singular, and this un-doing of the Aught is also the reason why it has to be idealistic. For idealism, with its denial of everything that distinguishes the singular from the All, is the tool of the philosopher's trade. With it, philosophy continues to work over the recalcitrant material until the later finally offers no more resistance to the smoke screen of the one-and-all concepts. If once all were woven into this mist, death would indeed be swallowed up, if not into the eternal triumph, at least into the one and universal night of the Nought. And here lies the ultimate conclusion of this wisdom: death would be—nothing' (Rosenzweig 2005: 10).
3. 'This movement falls, it is true, within the ethical community, and has this for its End; death is the fulfilment and the supreme "work" which the individual as such undertakes on its behalf' (Hegel 1977: 270).
4. Truth is always 'on the way'; it is not yet finished and over and done with. Rather, it is that which is constantly becoming; in other words: 'subjectivity is truth' (Kierkegaard 2009b: 171). This 'way' of truth is the accentuation of the 'how' over the 'what': it is verbal, infinitive and indicative, and not predicative. '*The objective accent fall on what is said, the subjective on how it is said*' (ibid.: 170; Kierkegaard's italics). The 'what' constitutes the doctrine of Christianity, while 'how' is the becoming Christian through inward deepening. 'Being a Christian is subjectively defined in this way: the decision rests in the subject; the appropriation is the paradoxical inwardness that differs specifically from all other inwardness. Being a Christian is defined not by the "what" of Christianity but by the "how" of the Christian. This "how" can go with only one thing, the absolute paradox . . . faith is the objective uncertainty with the repulsion of the absurd, held fast in the passion of inwardness, which precisely is the relation of inwardness raised to the highest power' (ibid.: 574).
5. 'Christianity has proclaimed itself as the eternal, essential truth that has come about in time; it has proclaimed itself as the paradox and has demanded the inwardness of faith in respect of what is stumbling block to the Jews and foolishness to the Greeks, and to the understanding the absurd' (Kierkegaard 2009b: 179). And again: 'what is paradoxically edifying therefore corresponds to the definition of God in time as an individual human being; for if that be the case, the individual relates to something outside himself. The paradox is precisely that this cannot be thought' (ibid.: 470).
6. 'The actuality of the suffering means the essential persistence and is its essential relation to the religious life' (Kierkegaard 2009b: 373). 'Suffering in connection with aesthetic and ethical existence is accidental; it can be absent and yet the mode of existence still be aesthetic and ethical, or if it acquires a deeper meaning here, it will be an element of transition. Otherwise here, where suffering is posited as something crucial for a religious existence, and just for that reason as definitive of inwardness: the more the suffering, the more religious existence, and the suffering persists' (ibid.: 241).
7. 'Everything subjective, which due to its dialectical inwardness eludes a direct form of expression, is an essential secret' (Kierkegaard 2009b: 67).

Chapter 3

Conflagration

Critique of historical reason

Like (and yet opposed to) Marx's atheistic political eschatology, Kierkegaard's Christian political eschatology is an eschatological delegitimation of the worldly power on theological foundation: what occurs here, in Marx as much as in Kierkegaard, is the 'critique' (not in a Kantian sense, but in the sense of 'delegitimation') of that historical reason which arose at the wake of Enlightenment (see Löwith 1991). With the Hegelian transformation of the Kantian empty form of time into the world-historical process of reason – reason that has become now 'processual', and thus has become more 'cunning' – the 'reconciliation' (achieved through dialectical 'mediation') between the *Weltgeschichte* (profane history) and *Heilsgeschichte* (sacred history) is supposed to have become complete (in the sense of *Vollendung*: completion as much as termination; one can also call it 'epochal': dated and fulfilled, closed and accomplished at the same time), according to Hegel's own claim, and in accordance to the demand of his 'philosophy of history'. For Hegel, this absolute point of mediation or synthesis is achieved on the cross, on that 'speculative Good Friday': this is indeed the *work* of the cross (Hegel 1988: 191)! The cross crosses, has already crossed, the abyss between knowledge and faith, the abyss that the Kantian transcendental philosophy set open once more. The reason that has crossed this abyss, and by its work of 'absolute negativity' has rendered itself into a 'speculative proposition' (Hegel 1977) thereby, has thought itself to have successfully taken away the apocalyptic sting of the sacred. Hegel's speculative philosophy of history does not know, even though merely formal, the 'infinite task' of Kantian teleological history:

God now sojourns on earth like Odysseus, and 'incarnates' himself on the successive forms of world-historical reason which, in the objective sense, are the world-political states and civilisations. Voltaire's 'philosophy of history' becomes, in Hegel's dialectical movement of mediation and synthesis, a 'theodicy':

> Hegel believes that, as a Christian philosopher, he can answer this question by secularising the Christian doctrine of providence and converting the salvation story of Christianity into a secular theodicy, for which the divine spirit is immanent in the world, the state is an earthly god and all history is divine. (Löwith 1991: 216)

With this inoperation of the apocalyptic sting – that apocalyptic sting which used to put the violence of the historical reason in question – now the deified order of the world-historical regimes has become, at least in principle in Hegel's metaphysical thought, totalitarian and violent. There is no longer anything to put into question the violence of history. Hegel's 'Christianity' which is suspicious of all illusions of transcendence has ended up in a new mode of 'legitimation' (as Carl Schmitt in his *Political Theology* of 1922 reminds us), a new pantheism of historical reason that sees the world-historical orders as various *figurations* of the absolute.

In two very different ways, both Nietzsche and Kierkegaard were attentive to this new mode of *figuration* that fundamentally appeals to that event of the God-becoming-man some 1800 years previously. Thus Nietzsche could write in one of his *Untimely Meditations*, namely, 'On the Uses and Disadvantages of History for Life':

> Such a point of view has accustomed the Germans to talk of a 'world process' and to justify their own age as the necessary result of this world-process; such a point of view has set history, insofar as history is 'the concept that realizes itself', 'the dialectics of the spirit of the peoples', and the 'world-tribunal', in place of the other spiritual powers, art and religion, as the sole sovereign power. (Nietzsche 1997: 104)

Similarly Kierkegaard accuses Hegel that he has 'deified the established order' (Kierkegaard 2004: 74):

> But that the established order has become something divine or is regarded as divine constitutes a falsehood which is made possible only by ignoring its origin. When a bourgeois has become a nobleman he is eager to make every effort to have his *vita ante acta* forgotten. So it is with the established order. It began with the God-relationship of the individual; but now this must be forgotten, the bridge hewn down, the established order deified. (Ibid.)

Both for Nietzsche and Kierkegaard, this deification has something decisive to do with 'Christianity'. While Nietzsche genealogically traces the origin of this theodicy of history back to the institutional impulses of Paul, and wants to rejuvenate the degenerate life of the West – and his own sick life – by bypassing this event of institution back to the Pre-Christian and Pre-Socratic tragic age of the Greeks, Kierkegaard gives up illusions of all immanence altogether (thus setting himself against the possible Nietzschean and Marxist revolutionary paths), and seeks to 'reintroduce Christianity into the Christendom' by bypassing, in the quantum leap of faith, the 1,800 years of its history. 'Christendom has done away with Christianity', writes Kierkegaard, 'without being quite aware of it. The consequence is that, if anything is to be done, one must try again to introduce Christianity into Christendom' (ibid.: 31).

> The deification of the established order is the secularization of everything . . . (instead) it is precisely this God-relationship of the individual which must put every established order in suspense, so that God, at any instance He will, by pressure upon the individual has immediately in his God-relationship a witness, a reporter, a spy, or whatever you prefer to call it, one who in unconditional obedience, by persecution, suffering, and death, puts the established order in suspense. (Ibid.: 77–8)

This 'Christian' character of Kierkegaardian eschatological suspension of the established order distinguishes itself from the 'atheistic' presuppositions of both Nietzsche and Marx, but what is common among them, despite this fundamental difference, is the emphasis upon the individual and individuation that is irreducible to the totality, to the tyrannical order of anonymous universality called 'the state' or 'the Church':

> The established order desires to be totalitarian, recognizing nothing over it, but having under it every individual, and judging every individual who is integrated in it. And 'that individual', who expounds the most humble, but at the same time the most humane doctrine about what it means to be a man, the established order desires to terrify by imputing him the guilt of blasphemy. (Ibid.: 78)

The essence of Kierkegaard's eschatology can be grasped in these concrete and concentrated formulations. To reintroduce Christianity into Christendom means to introduce judgement upon history, history that Kierkegaard names as 'Christendom' (thus separating it from 'Christianity'). Christ is not judged by history but 'it is He that is the examiner. His life is the examination and that not alone for that race and generation, but for the whole race' (ibid.: 29). He is 'the judge who condemns the established order': herein lies his 'absolute isolation from the established order, His aloofness from everything that has to do with it' (ibid.: 43). To introduce Christianity into Christendom is to bring the whole history of Christendom of 1,800 years to a sudden halt, to bring it dialectically to its standstill, 'for a halt which is the condition for the very existence of faith: thou art brought to a halt by the possibility of the offense' (ibid.: 35). This standing still is the very standing still of understanding: 'the God-Man is the paradox, absolutely the paradox; hence it is quite clear that the understanding must come to a standstill before it' (ibid.: 70). Since 'the absolute seeks only the eternal', 'at the absolute the understanding stands still' (ibid.: 106). The understanding stands still because the absolute is an offence: it is the scandal and the foolishness of crucifixion which passes this absolute judgement upon the violence of the world-historical sovereigns who rule by force and not by love:

> Whenever the understanding stands still in this wise, there is the possibility of offense. If now there is to be victorious advance, faith must be present, for faith is a new life. Without faith a man remains offended and then perhaps he becomes something great in the world . . . the possibility of offense consists precisely in the fact that it is the believer who is regarded by the world as a criminal. (Ibid.)

To introduce Christianity into Christendom is to suspend the order of *nomos*, the order of worldly sovereignties, and replace it by the mystery of suffering. While Christianity in its original impulse – Kierkegaard calls it 'contemporaneity' – has this essential relation to suffering, the 1,800 years of Christendom has transformed this mystery into vulgar triumph. To reintroduce Christianity means to reintroduce the original abyss of suffering that the cross once and for all, offensively, opened from the heart of the world. This means that the speculative dialectics of the world-historical process (through which the Hegelian figure of the Absolute Spirit continuously progresses on the homogenous plane) has to be replaced by a new dialectic, a 'negative dialectic' or by a thought of difference without dialectics, a thought that is seized by the absolute paradox that 'in the world truth conquers only by suffering' (ibid.: 175) and that 'truth is persecuted' (ibid.: 177). This means to reintroduce 'the heterogeneity of Christ' (ibid.: 181) with respect to all world-historical politics; this means to eschatologically render the established regimes in the profane historical order, including that of the Church, merely 'provisional':

> Christ says, 'one day at the end of time I shall come again'. This form of existence (if I may so express myself) makes the whole existence of the church here on earth a parenthesis, a parenthesis in Christ's life; the content of this parenthesis begins with Christ's Ascension, and with His second coming it ends. So here the case is not similar to every other historical relationship between an individual and others who profit as a matter of course by his victory, for neither is such an individual the pattern, nor is such an individual he that shall come again. It is only Christ that makes His life a test for all men. When He ascends up to heaven the examination period begins;

it has lasted 1,800 years, it will perhaps last 18,000. But He is coming again. And if this is so, then all direct adherence to Him, with the aim of profiting by His triumph as a matter of course, is more impossible than in the case of any other men. (Ibid.: 181)

This 'eschatological reserve' makes all economy – profit and gain, investment and return – of worldly sovereignty impossible.

> Worldliness is eager to embellish itself as godliness, and in this case God and Emperor are blended together in the question, as if these two had obviously and directly something to do with each other, as if perhaps they were rivals of one another, and as if God were a sort of Emperor – that is to say, the question takes God in vain and secularises Him. But Christ draws the distinction, the infinite distinction . . . (Ibid.: 153)

Hegel's secular theodicy of history, even though its foundation lies in the *theologia crucis* inspired by Luther, takes the name of God in vain: for Christianity as the eschatological event par excellence – namely, the event of the exultation of Christ, the *parousia* in his second coming – Hegel transforms by the cunning of his 'speculative Good Friday' into an occurrence in the intra-mundane theatre of existing world-historical politics. Christianly speaking, Christ's exultation is eschatological – that is, in eternity, while his whole life in the temporal order of world-history is suffering: 'suffering is all the greater and more intense in proportion to the loftiness' (ibid.: 174). What, then, is erased in Christendom (that from which the Hegelian theodicy of history draws its speculative meaning) is that of the absolute disjunction: this either/or refuses the speculative investment in the meaning of the profane history and to draw economic profit from it. 'Christianity is the absolute, has only one mode of being, namely absolute being; if it is not absolute, it is abolished; in relation to Christianity either/or applies absolutely' (ibid.: 205).

To reintroduce Christianity into Christendom is, then, to reintroduce that eschatological disjunction, that kenotic Christological separation, that finds no manifestation in the history of the Church. Kierkegaard this way distinguishes, by an intensification of difference once more, between the historical element of Christianity and the 1,800 years history of Christendom.

> It is important above all that there be fixed an unshakeable qualitative difference between *the historical element in Christianity* (the paradox that the eternal came into existence once in time) and the history of Christianity, the history of its followers, etc. The fact that God came into existence in human form under the Emperor Augustus: that is the historical element in Christianity, the historical in a paradoxical composition. (Kierkegaard 1994: 161)

Kierkegaard, then, goes on to say:

> The Christian fact has no history, for it is the paradox that God once came into existence in time. This is the offense, but also the point of departure; and whether this was eighteen hundred years ago or yesterday, one can just as well be contemporary with it. Like the polar star this paradox never changes its position and therefore has no history, so this paradox stands immovable and unchanged; and though Christianity were to last another ten thousand years, one would get no further from this paradox than the contemporaries were. For the distance is not to be measured by the quantitative scale of time and space, for it is qualitatively decisive by the fact that it is a paradox. (Ibid.: 163)

In *Training in Christianity* Kierkegaard develops this distinction more explicitly in Johannine spirit than in the line of the Pauline polemical theology of *Romans*: the distinction between truth and truths, between the way and the result, between life and the doctrine (the latter constitutes the dogma of the established Church): 'Jesus saith unto him, I am the way, the truth, and the life: no man cometh unto the Father, but by me' (John 14: 6). The eschatological suspension of the established order of the world, the world that is ruled by *nomos* and not by *pistis*, introduces that intensification of difference, that absolute distinction between Christianity and Christendom, between the militant Church and the established Church. This kenotic eschatology of Kierkegaard is also Christological. Christ himself draws this 'absolute disjunction':

> What Christ said about His kingdom not being of this world was not said with special reference to those times when He uttered this saying; it is an eternally valid utterance about the relation of Christ's kingdom to this world, and so it is valid for every age. As soon as Christ's kingdom comes to terms with the world, Christianity is abolished. If, on the other hand, Christ is the truth, His is truly enough a kingdom in this world, but not of this world, that is to say, it is militant. (Kierkegaard 2004: 190)

This utterance of Christ being 'valid for all ages': this is the offence and scandal for historical reason. The truth of this statement has nothing to do with the truth of the world (see Henry 2002). Rather, the truth of this statement comes to undo the truths of the world: 'in this world there can be question only of a church militant' (Kierkegaard 2004: 188). This truth of Christ's statement, Christ himself being the truth, is then a polemical truth, truth as *polemos*: undoing, contending, contesting infinitely the truths of the world. Kierkegaard here wants us to attend the verbal infinitude of the Johannine reporting of Christ's remark: it is the truth 'infinitely', the truth being the truth of the way (or, the way being the truth), that is, truth 'in the process of becoming' against the truths of the world that simply don't become (ibid.: 189).

> For in this world Christ's church can truly survive only by contending, that is, by fighting for its survival every instant. If it is the established church, this implies that it has triumphed. The militant church survives only by contending, and the church which is called established must surely by one which survives after it has triumphed. (Ibid.: 190)

We must intensify the qualitative disjunction between the truth and truths. The truth of the world does not consist of the truths of the world; it can't be staged on the theatre of world-historical politics:

> they have quite forgotten that Christ's life on earth is sacred history, which must not be confounded with the history of the human race or of the world. They have entirely forgotten that the God-man is essentially heterogeneous from every other individual man and from the race as a whole. They have entirely forgotten that Christianity is essentially related to eternity, that life have on earth is the time of probation for every individual in particular among the countless millions who have lived or shall live. (Ibid.: 199–200)

In this difference between truth and truths lies the difference between the truth as the way and life[1] (as the apostle John expounds) and truths of the doctrines of the established Church, between the militant Church and the triumphant Church, between the sacred history (*Heilsgeschichte*) and the profane history (*Weltgeschichte*). Here is the political theology of Kierkegaard, drawn upon the Johannine conception of 'the way' and 'life', now transformed into an existential eschatology:

> Christ was the truth, He was the way, or He was the way in the sense that the truth is the way. The fact that He has travelled the way to the end does not alter anything in the situation of the successor, who, if he is of the truth and desires to be of the truth, can be so only by following 'the way' . . . so there is no occasion or opportunity for triumphing; for only he who has followed the way to the end could triumph, but he is no longer in this world. He has gone up on high, as Christ also was the way when He ascended up to heaven. (Ibid.: 187–8)

Similarly,

> Christ was the truth [in his humiliation] and is the truth . . . it is as essential 'for the truth' to suffer in this world as to triumph in another world, the world of truth – and Christ Jesus is the same in His humiliation as in His exultation. (Ibid.: 138)

It is the same Christ who is humiliated and who is, or who will be exulted: *kenosis* is glory! But in the order of *Weltgeschichte* this – that *kenosis* is glory! – can appear only *incognito*:[2] glory remains an *absconditus* in the profane order of the world-historical politics. Therefore, the sacred history is also a history of the secret: we can't decipher or decrypt its sense at the manifested order of aesthetics and politics. What is left, then, is that un-aesthetic, ugly, disfigured Christ, hanging on the cross, his eyes empty sockets, and his blood oozing out from his wounds: a sight that offends us, must offend us, as it offended 1,800 years earlier (see Hengel 1977), a scandal and utter foolishness on the part of the Messiah. 'Such is the relationship between exultation and lowliness. The humiliation of the true Christian is not plain humiliation, it is merely the reflected image of exultation, but the reflection of it in this world, where exultation must appear conversely as lowliness and humiliation' (Kierkegaard 2004: 179).

A dialectic qualitatively different from the speculative dialectic of Hegel: the cross is still the stake, but its meaning is no more 'speculative'. The 'reflection' of the exultation is not repetition of the same but a qualitative disjunction, an eruption of heterogeneity no longer assimilable to the unitary hypothesis of 'thought and being', an offence to understanding that the world can no longer digest: the *absconditus* remains unthought and unthinkable, a paradox which is not part of any speculative truth, an abomination that eternally refuses to be a simple disclosure of the world as it exists. The humiliation is an index, a pointer, a cipher whose *telos* does not form the form of the world as it exists but a form of the world that is *to come*: it is an eschatological potentiality that makes all present forms of the world exposed open to the judgement that always comes in the name of an unconditional justice, or love. The form of the world, then, as it exists, is not an autochthonous and aboriginal being, lacking justice and love. Therefore, exultation can appear here only as humiliation, glory as suffering. To confound the two, to have taken away the eschatological sting of judgement, to neutralise the bitterness of the paradox, to liquidate the scandal of the cross and its offence: this is what 1,800 years of Christendom has done, and this is what Hegel's speculative dialectic precisely has accomplished. But this is to deny precisely 'the way', 'the truth' and 'life' of Christianity; that is: its heterogeneity in respect to the form of the world, at any given instance of time, as it exists. As Christendom has done away with the mystery of suffering and replaced it with triumph, it has ended up becoming an apology of the world as it exists and no longer a Church militant, a Church that offends. 'Christianity came into the world', Kierkegaard writes, 'as the absolute – not for consolation, humanely understood; on the contrary, it speaks again and again of the sufferings which a Christian must endure, or which a man must endure to become and to be a Christian, sufferings he can well avoid merely by refraining from becoming a Christian' (ibid.: 58).

Where lies the offence of Christianity? It lies in its 'collision with the established order' (ibid.: 93); in the kenotic mode of God's being on earth (a servant, dying as a criminal on the cross); that an individual can claim to be God; and to be a Christian, to follow Christ to the cross, giving up all economy of return, of profit and gain. All economy – the very economy of the worldly order – constitutes itself on the logic of symmetry; the divine economy, on the other hand, is an economy which one cannot hope to invest it: it can only be a hope against hope, and hope against all hopelessness, a hope without economy; it is a hope on the radical dissymmetry that undoes the truths of the world, and keeps the world open to the advenient par excellence, the second coming. We must, then, be able to distinguish between the historical elements of this divine economy (the sacred history) and the history of the worldly economy (the world-history), 'for Christ's life on earth, sacred history, stands for itself alone outside history' (ibid.: 59):

> 'History', says faith, 'has nothing whatever to do with Christ. As applying to Him, we have only sacred history (qualitatively different from history in general), which recounts the story of His life under the conditions of His humiliation, and reports moreover that He himself said that He was God. He is the paradox, which history can never digest or convert into a common syllogism. In His humiliation He is the same as in His exultation – but the 1,800 years (or if there are 18,000 of them) have nothing whatever to do with the case. The brilliant consequences in world history which well nigh convince even a professor of history that he was God – these brilliant consequences are surely not His return in glory! But this is really about what they mean by it: it appears here again that they make out Christ to be a man whose return in glory can be nothing more than the consequences of His life in history – whereas Christ's return in glory is something entirely different, something that is believed.' (Ibid.: 25)

That 'professor of history' is none other than Hegel: here, as elsewhere, the similarity and yet opposition to something like Nietszchean polemics is striking. Like Nietzsche's 'untimely meditations' which is a 'deconstruction' and a diagnosis of the sickness of history (Nietzsche the great diagnostician!), here is the Kierkegaardian diagnostics and 'deconstruction' of the sickness of historical reason. However, unlike Nietzsche, the therapeutics offered here is faith in the sacred history that is a divine economy (without economy!) with a qualitative disjunction: Nietzschean 'untimeliness' (Nietzsche does not hesitate to call it 'eternity') here meets the 'untimeliness' (Kierkegaard explicitly and Christianly calls it 'eternity') of Kierkegaard (Nietzsche knew Kierkegaard and even mentions Kierkegaard's name once; one does not know however whether the reverse is also the case). At stake here is precisely this: the indigestible paradox of Christ is unassimilable to the deification of the established order. The divinity of Christ is not a predicate or attribute of the world-history, nor is it its foundation; it cannot be deduced as a consequence of His life:

'humiliation (the fact it pleases God, to be the lowly man) is therefore something He Himself has joined together, something He wills to have knit together, a dialectical knot which no one shall presume to untie . . .' (ibid.: 28). What, then, is irreducible to historical knowledge and to knowledge as such – such is the incomprehensible paradox! – is the facticity of *kenosis*. God's *kenosis* on the cross is reducible neither to any logical-conceptual attribute of a logical-doctrinal system nor to any empirical fact. God's *kenosis* thus marks the irreducibility of sacred history:

> he who believes it must be contemporary with Him in His humiliation. When God chooses to let Himself be born in lowly station, when He who holds all possibilities in His hand clothes Himself in the form of a servant, when He goes about defenceless and lets men do with Him as they will. (Ibid.: 29)

In Hegel's immanent theodicy of history (and in Christendom at large), it is this 'tension of the paradox [that] was relaxed', 'without in the least noticing the possibility of offense' (ibid.: 30). The absolute, then, becomes a figure of world-history: the unconditional, then (which is the true 'measuring rod' of history, Christianly speaking), is *eo ipso* abolished. What is, thus, abolished is the immeasurable 'measuring rod' – the unconditional par excellence – whereby the violence of history can be put into question. Here is, then, the absolute paradox: what puts the violence of history into question is not the divine sovereignty directly appearing itself in his full sovereign power but the infinite, divine compassion and abandonment of all powers – His *kenosis*. That the unconditional is the sacrifice, sacrifice of all sacrifices: this is the crucifixion of understanding:

> The unconditional, everything that applies the measuring rod of the unconditional, is *eo-ipso* a sacrifice. For though it is true enough that men wish to exercise compassion and self-denial and want to have wisdom, etc., yet they wish to determine for themselves the measure, insisting that it shall be only *to a certain degree*; they are not desirous of abolishing all these glorious virtues; on the contrary they would be at a good bargain and without inconvenience have the experience of practising them. Hence the true divine compassion is unconditionally a sacrifice as soon as it manifests itself in the world. It comes in compassion for man, and it is man who treads it underfoot. (Ibid.: 53)

The abandonment exercised in the order of the worldliness is never the unconditional: it 'never goes beyond a certain degree' (ibid.: 54). Halfway it is bargained and assimilated once again into the conditioned order of economic transaction, of practical negotiations, of what Kierkegaard simply calls 'politics'. The conditioned order of worldly politics does not know the immeasurable measure of justice or love: it does not know abandonment (*hensynsløs*). On the contrary, the divine *hensynsløs* is truly unconditional and, thereby, it exceeds all conditioned negotiations of world-historical politics: '*to make oneself literally one with the most miserable* (and this, this alone is divine compassion) is for men the "too much"' (ibid.; Kierkegaard's italics). The *abandon* is unbearable and unthinkable; it is 'sublime': 'the fact is, this is so sublime that one cannot bear to see it in daily use; to bear it one must have it at a distance' (ibid.).

What is unthinkable, then, is not so much His divine sovereignty but His weakness, His compassion and abandonment, for it makes every worldly order ruled by *potestas* delegitimate: the cross is abomination, not because it manifests in full form the divine force but because it pours unto the world the divine abandonment. It is in this sense Kierkegaard could say: 'thus christianly understood, exultation is in this world humiliation . . . the exultation is humiliation, or that humiliation is the true exultation' (ibid.: 235). To have faith, which is another thing than to have knowledge (for faith is the way, truth and life, to understand it in Johannine way), is to be *contemporaneous* with this humiliation, with this compassion and abandonment; it is not the participation in the profit of exultation *sans* humiliation. The economy of human knowledge, the economy of the worldly order of earthly sovereignties which rules by the law and not by love, wants to participate in the exultation of Christ (which is only an eschatological event, the event of the 'beyond') *sans* humiliation. This is what Dietrich Bonhoeffer justly calls 'cheap grace' as set against the 'costly grace' (Bonhoeffer 1995) of the disciples.[3] On the other hand, to be a Christian – to be a disciple – is costly, as exemplified by martyrs and apostles in their very life and way, but even they in no way can approximate the divine compassion of the Christ dying on the cross. Christians, the true Christians, are not the admirers of the exulted Christ; on the other hand, the 'Christians' of Christendom, like Bishop Mynster of Copenhagen, are admirers of the exulted Christ whom they reduce to an aesthetic, glorious figure of triumph in the worldly order of Christendom. These admirers are 'adherents of a doctrine' of the established Church; Christians are, on other hand, 'followers of a life' of the one who died on the cross out of infinite compassion (Kierkegaard 2004: 215). The 'followers of a life', who are on the way, and who live in truth, are the militant ones who associate themselves 'with Christ in His humiliation, although drawn to Him on high' (ibid.: 210). Eighteen hundred years of Christendom can neither prove nor disprove the validity of such a life, such a way, such a truth, unless the individual – and the individual can alone have this – becomes 'contemporary with Him in his humiliation':

> It is this Jesus Christ in His humiliation who spoke these words. And you have no right to apply to yourself one word of Christ's, not a single word,

you have not the least part in Him, no society with Him in the remotest way, unless you have become so contemporary with Him in his humiliation that, exactly like His immediate contemporaries, you must take heed of His warning: 'Blessed is he whosoever shall not be offended in me.' (Ibid.: 32)

What does it mean to be contemporary? The radical difference of this *kenotic* eschatology – that is, to be 'contemporary with Him in his humiliation' – from the Hegelian theodicy of history is again strikingly manifest. In the Hegelian dialectical schema of the theodicy of world-history, each civilisation or state has its own time of its destinal participation in the universal history that is constantly moved ahead by the irresistible storm of progress to its *telos*; to be contemporary means for Hegel this participation in the destinal manifestation of the Absolute Spirit as world history. To embody the Absolute Spirit in its own allotted epochal moment, for each civilisation, is to be contemporary with the Absolute Spirit at that stage of its unfolding. Each epochal moment of its manifestation is, thus, necessarily incomplete and unfulfilled; only at the end of history when there is no longer anything left for the spirit to 'phenomenalise' itself – for history, for Hegel, is always history of the manifestation of the absolute (this path being the 'way of despair', as Hegel (1977: 49) describes it) – only then (and this has occurred in Hegel's own time) does the spirit come to its *pleroma*, which also marks the very termination of its 'movement'.

This grand secularisation of eschatology in Hegel's theodicy ends up confounding the sacred history with the profane history, the result being the apology of the world as it exists. The world-conformism of the secular eschatology lies in the normative obligation that is imposed upon the individual – who is grasped here only as a mere particular instantiation of the universal, and not in his or her absolute singularity – that s/he be 'contemporary' (to be in 'sync') with the universal spirit, as embodied in the realm of the world-historical politics, at that moment and at that stage of its manifestation. This order of the world-history is nothing other than the history of the human race, or the universal spirit:[4] it is the successive appearing of civilisations on the stage of universal history where each one fulfils its appointed task, and then it becomes 'stale' and disappears. God – the God who becomes man – is forced to appear in this voyage of spirit where civilisations engage with each other in bloody 'life and death' struggles to appear on the stage of universal history. Hegel seeks to draw from this theodicy of history the very meaning of redemption, now in its secularised version, and forces individuals to participate in this metaphysical violence of the historical reason. The absolute paradox that Christ is God, the God who in his very humiliation passes judgement upon history – and hence, in that sense, He is outside history altogether – is now completely liquidated in the Absolute Knowledge.

> If, on the contrary, one begins with the assumption (the assumption of faith) that he was God, one has thereby cancelled, annulled, the 1,800 years as having nothing to do with the case, proving nothing *pro* nor *contra*, inasmuch as the certitude of faith is something infinitely higher. And it is in one or other of these ways one must begin. If one begins in the latter way, everything is as it 'should be'. (Kierkegaard 2004: 21–2)

If one assumes the (Hegelian) Absolute Knowledge as the very meaning of revelation and redemption (the whole economy of spirit manifesting itself on the immanent plane of world-historical politics), then the paradox, in all its offence, disappears: the result is Christendom. On the other hand, if the assumption is that of the certitude of Christian faith, then one has to bypass 1,800 years of the history of Christendom so as to be contemporary with the Christ event on the cross. This paradox of faith here, the paradox of being truly contemporaneous with the Christ event, is that it demands to be non-contemporary with the contemporary world (that is, to be non-contemporary with Christendom that has come as the result and consequences of its 1,800 years of history). Thus, to be contemporary in accordance to the assumption of Absolute Knowledge is a radically, and qualitatively, different thing, an altogether different thing, than to be contemporary in accordance to the assumption of faith. Only by virtue of this paradox, with its absolute event of crucifixion which has set apart the world from its foundation – the very experience of the holy (*das Heilige*), can Christianity rise up as the radical protest against the violence of the world, 'instead of joining forces with the established order and as a reformer bettering it, or as the expected One raising it to its highest potency' (ibid.: 43):

> For in relation to the absolute there is only one tense: the present. For whom who is not contemporary with the absolute – for him it has no existence. And as Christ is the absolute, it is easy to see that with respect to Him there is only one situation: that of contemporaneousness. The five, the seven, the fifteen, the eighteen hundred years are neither here nor there; they do not change Him, neither do they in any wise reveal who He was, for he who he is is revealed only to faith. (Ibid.: 58)

Kierkegaard goes on to say:

> For what true Christians there are in each generation are contemporary with Christ, have nothing to do with Christians of former generations, but everything to do with the contemporary Christ. His earthly life accompanies the race, and accompanies every generation, as the eternal history; His earthly life possesses the eternal contemporaneousness. (Ibid.: 59)

This sacred history with its 'eternal contemporaneousness' cannot be translated into direct communication without taking away its paradox and its offence, that is, without violence to it: this is why 'the possibility of the offense belongs essentially to the experience of faith' (ibid.: 92). This is why we need *maieutic* discourse, the dialectic of communication of a qualitatively different sort (or, rather, a non-dialectical discourse of difference), rather than the Hegelian speculative dialectics that pretends to be, or aims to be, a discourse of direct communication. Christendom has transformed the indirect communication into direct communication, thereby transforming Christ into a doctrine, taking away the offence and the paradox. Christendom in the 1,800 years of its profane history deduces its triumph as consequences from Christ's life on earth (this is the project in which Hegel as much as the contemporary Hegelians in Copenhagen participated); but what is taken away here is the very 'cost of discipleship': 'in the situation of contemporaneousness, when one could ascertain at any instance how far the disciple's life resembled the Master's, no world-historical hocus–pocus was possible, the disciple was constituted in accordance with the paradigm' (ibid.: 94). To follow Christ, that is, to be Christian, demands that the follower her-/himself has to be *kenotic*: s/he must follow the Master to the cross on Golgotha; s/he 'must go through lowliness and humiliation' (ibid.: 216): this kenotic eschatology of Kierkegaard is a cry far removed from the triumphal march of the world-historical spirit that Hegel so majestically dramatised. At stake here is Kierkegaard's eschatological 'critique' of historical reason, and in this sense his is similar, though in an opposed manner, to Nietzschean genealogical deconstruction of 'history'. It is an illusion of the philosophy of history based upon the ideology of progress that 'with the amendment to the constitution, with the fourth estate, with all men wishing to solve the problem of likeness and equality between man and man in the medium of worldliness, i.e. in the medium the nature of which is difference and inequality' (Kierkegaard 1994: 297).

Franz Rosenzweig's great messianic deconstruction of the Hegelian triumphal ideology of progress is not far from here, as is clear from Rosenzweig's own explicit acknowledgement of both Kierkegaard and Nietzsche. Both Kierkegaard and Rosenzweig agree that revelation and redemption are not events that occur on the immanent drama of the grand world-historical politics, and that they are not categories that belong to any system of mobile concepts. Religion – Christianity without Christendom for Kierkegaard and messianicity without messianism for Rosenzweig – is not a conceptual category; it can't be enclosed within any system of concepts, or assimilated within any system of the world, for it keeps our historical existence open to what is 'outside' the world from the heart of the world, to the infinity of 'the way', of 'truth' and of 'life'. That death is not the final facticity of human existence, and the law is not the ultimate horizon of life, but rather that death opens up a new life and that the law is made possible only in the demand of infinite justice: this excess, this infinity, outside any possible closures and enclosures, infinity from the heart of finitude – this is the stake of both Kierkegaardian and Rosenzweigian thinking. Both of them agree with Nietzsche that it is the individual in his or her singularity, and not as a particular instantiation of the universal, which opens up the very possibility of thinking redemption anew, a new universal redemption for each and every one of us living at the end of time, as it were.

Critique of the contemporary age of reflection

Kierkegaard's eschatological vision of the suspension of the established order – these 1,800 years of Christendom – is turned, in his short treatise called *The Present Age*, into a 'critique' of the contemporary age of reflection in a form that Karl Löwith calls 'anticommunist manifesto'.[5] The following lines read almost as if they are written for Marx:

> At the bottom of all relationships between man and man qua man it is only possible to think that the differences lie within the identity of immanence, that is, within the essential equality. The one man cannot be thought to be different from all others by reason of a specific equality – otherwise all thinking ceases, as it quite consistently does in the paradox religious sphere or the sphere of faith . . . but between God and man there is an eternal, essential, qualitative difference . . . between God and man there is and remains an eternal, essential, qualitative difference. *The paradox-religious situation comes to evidence when God appoints a particular man to have divine authority – nota bene* in relation to what was entrusted to him. (Kierkegaard 1994: 207; Kierkegaard's italics)

Like Nietzsche, Kierkegaard here poses himself as the genius-diagnostician of the contemporary historical culture. And the method too is more or less the same: to diagnose, through a symptomatologic analysis, that sovereign hegemonic phantasm that constitutes and sickens the body-historic of the contemporary epoch. The sovereign principle – which Reiner Schürmann calls *arché* – of his contemporary Christendom is diagnosed as nothing other than a phantom, hardly of any ontological value and solidity, but for that matter overwhelmingly powerful and totalising. Kierkegaard calls this sovereign phantasm 'the public', which is no one and everyone, a pure virtuality without limit, and without the measure of actuality: in the epoch of modernity where every bit of religion is attempted to be secularised, including the unbearable scandal of the cross, the *hegemonikon* of the public is the new legitimising principle of the contemporary world-order. With the withering away of the monarchy which was supported by the feudal system of political economy, the 'monstrous nonentity' of the public has now become the new 'theological ground' of the world-political order. With the withering away of the one monarch in place (which is the very definition of 'monarchy': *mono-arché*), the public is a new mode of legitimation of the established order where everyone now behaves like a monarch in turn. 'Composed of someones such as these, of individuals in moments when they are nobodies, the public is a kind of colossal something, an abstract void and vacuum that is all and nothing' (Kierkegaard 2009c: 97). The secret *arché* of this world-conformism is difficult to decipher, for it manifests itself precisely as what it is not. Hence it is necessary to develop a rigorous science of symptomatology:

> A passionate, tumultuous age wants to overthrow everything, set aside everything. An age that is revolutionary but also reflecting and devoid of passion changes the expression of power into a dialectical *tour de force: it lets everything remain but subtly drains the meaning out of it; rather than culminating in an uprising, it exhausts the inner actuality of relations in a tension of reflection that lets everything remain and yet has transformed the whole of existence into an equivocation that in its facticity is – while entirely privately a dialectical fraud interpolates a secret way of reading – that it is not.* (Ibid.: 77; Kierkegaard's italics)

What is necessary is a new phenomenology to phenomenalise the phantasm that constitutes and yet is hidden in the order of constituted phenomenality, for the phantasm is no 'being' and yet, no mere 'nothing'. The overwhelming power of this nonentity (such is the power of phantasm!) is a new mythic economy, namely: 'reflection' or 'speculation'. Like Nietzsche, Kierkegaard too is acutely attentive to the economy of speculative investment and the return of reflection on the immanent plane of self-presence that totalises the world at the epoch of modernity: this is the economy that constantly returns to the self-same, via investment (which Hegel calls 'diremption'), as the vicious circular return of the capital with interest. The endless 'web of reflection' is a speculative investment which with its endless cunning incorporates all individuals into its prison-house. Only 'religious inwardness' can interrupt – by its de-cision (*decidere*: to cut off, to separate, to disjoin, to divorce) – this vicious circular return of the same. This 'web of reflection' is the new mythic foundation of all modern forms of totalitarianism: the 'generation' triumphing over the 'individual'; the reduction of singularity into quantitative differences; liquidation of 'the qualitative disjunction'; the subsumption of singular beings under the homogeneous order of unity; massification by levelling and constituting, by the force of violence, anonymous order of totality, etc. 'Just as one computes the diagonal in a parallelogram of forces, so also can the law of levelling be computed, for the individual who levels others, is himself carried away, and so on' (ibid.: 86). The tyranny of this anonymous and phantasmal order of totality lacks all measure and limit in the profane order of worldly existence; only 'with respect to the eternal' (ibid.: 89) does this omnipresent levelling prove to be 'impotent'. This breakthrough of the eternal into the immanent order of worldly existence can only be an 'anticommunist manifesto', a radical protest against all immanentisation of God into an intra-mundane existence, and against all deification of the world in turn ('The essential paradox is the protest against immanence' (Kierkegaard 2010a: 70)). In that sense, the epoch of modernity with all its levelling and secularisation, according to Kierkegaard, is a new form of pantheism and paganism. A radical de-cision to be possible, the endless and vicious 'web of reflection' has to be interrupted, and that which interrupts this vicious circle of speculative economy cannot be a mere higher potency of something that exists in the order of immanence. It has to be something radically and absolutely heterogeneous and dissymmetrical, irreducible to the mythic economy of return and continuum; it cannot be 'merely a higher potency within the identity' (ibid.: 74). This is why in the order of Christendom there is no decision, and since all ethical responsibility demands decision, unconditionally, the epoch of modernity is essentially an irresponsible historical existence.

'Whereas a passionate age accelerates, raises up and overthrows, elevates and debases, a reflective apathetic age does the opposite, it shifts and impedes, it levels' (Kierkegaard 2009c: 84). By neutralising elements of singularity and subsuming difference into speculative identity, the pantheistic immanence of the modern world makes events impossible to appear to it; instead what appears is the endless publicity and announcement of events that never come. In this evasion of responsibility lies our inability to acknowledge the historical character of its mode of being 'the world', the historicality which exceeds all forms of historicisms. In this sense, Karl Löwith is right to say that despite all protests against Hegel, Kierkegaard indeed engages with historical thinking, but this *historicality* is to be radically distinguished from Hegel's speculative history that writes grey upon the grey on the walls of world-history. What Kierkegaard calls 'event' which the passionate ages knew, and which no longer appears in the world now, is something qualitatively different from what Hegel means by the 'event' that falls in history. What Kierkegaard calls 'the event' is 'the qualitative expression of difference', a *spacing* of history, and a sublime disjunction of history from its deepest foundation. Linguistically speaking, Hegel's speculative 'grey upon grey' is like chatter; Hegel's philosophy of language is chatter, purely made of concepts, without true events and sense:

> What is it to chatter? It is the annulment of the passionate disjunction between being silent and speaking. Only the person who can remain essentially silent can speak essentially, can act essentially. Silence is inwardness, Chattering gets ahead of essential speaking, and giving utterance to reflection has a weakening effect on action by getting ahead of it. But the person who can speak essentially because he is able to keep silent will not have a profusion of things to speak about but one thing only, and he will find time to speak and to keep silent. (Ibid.: 97)

Chattering is irresponsible speaking: it cunningly evades responsibility and action 'by getting ahead of it'. Lacking 'the intensity of infinite enthusiasm' (ibid.: 111), which only the singular individual can have, the contemporary age of secularism (which overvalues the general, the public, the state or the Church) does not know what alone can be redemptive for it: 'the transparency of the event' (ibid.: 15) – 'the voice of God [which] is always a whisper' (ibid.: 10). Like Nietzsche, Kierkegaard refuses to call the ever recent and ever noisy occurrences in the world 'events', though they seem like events, given the publicity and announcements they receive. Like chattering, they emit more smoke rather than doing what they are supposed to do: to welcome the radically new life – which for Kierkegaard is the life of faith, understood in Johannine spirit – out of the singular, absolute and fundamental decision, in a responsible way.

Kierkegaard believes that only the religious inwardness can break the *hegemonikon* of modernity, for the inward deepening of faith by definition exceeds the irresponsibility of the hegemonic fantasm that is the public. And Kierkegaard understands this inwardness eschatologically as suffering and through suffering, as the singularisation of existence: this singularity infinitely exceeds all forms of empty universality, and puts into question the tyranny of the anonymous totalities. This de-cision is not the self-assertion of a sovereign figure; rather, it is the decision of faith, taken at the absolute moment of exception, by renouncing of all sovereign powers and the force of its law. The *nomos* of the world has its source in a sovereign phantasm, but this non-actuality is more powerful than any specific worldly powers; only in relation to eternity can the totalising violence of this tyranny be eschatologically brought to a halt. Then a new aeon begins. Kierkegaard calls it 'the fourth state': the world of sufferers and martyrs, and not that of worldly sovereign figures! Kierkegaard writes posthumously in one of his prefaces:

> For tyrants (in the form of emperors, Kings, Popes, Jesuits, generals, diplomats) have hitherto in a decisive moment been able to rule and direct the world; but from the time the fourth estate has come into the picture – when it has had time to settle itself in such a way that it is rightly understood – it will be seen that in the decisive moment only martyrs are able to rule

the world. That is, no man will be able to rule the human race in such a moment, only the Deity can do it with the help of absolutely obedient men who at the same time are willing to suffer – but such a man is the martyr. And when in an elder formation the decisive moment was overcome, then the ordinary worldly government took over; but from the moment fourth estate come into the picture it will be seen that even when the crisis has been overcome, it is not possible to govern in a *worldly* way. To rule in a worldly way, to be a ruler in the worldly sense, however much labour and responsibility is involved in it, is a pleasure . . . (Kierkegaard 1994: 300)

Kierkegaard goes on to say:

To be selected to be the ruler in a worldly sense is regarded as good fortune, but to be selected to serve as a ruler in a religious sense is, humanly speaking, rather like a punishment, in any case, humanly speaking, it is suffering, humanly speaking, it is the opposite of an advantage. (Ibid.: 301)

What is authority?

The proximity of Kierkegaardian 'political theology' to Schmittean 'political theology' is striking here: like Schmitt's apocalyptic 'critique' of the technology of politics in the epoch of secular-liberal modernity (modernity which has its hidden 'theological' ground on Hegel's pantheistic-immanent metaphysics),[6] Kierkegaard's apocalyptic critique turns against the new mode of legitimation which makes responsible 'decision' and responsibility as such impossible. What the present age lacks is the passionate intensity, the intensity of decision taken at the extreme limit of the 'normal' situation. As such, both Kierkegaard and Schmitt, though in two different ways, are the thinkers of 'the pain of actuality' (Kierkegaard 2009c: 15) that is founded upon an apocalyptic vision of history. While Kierkegaard welcomes this apocalyptic revolution in an 'anticommunist' manner (that is, not by worldly means of 'politics'), Schmitt is (as Jacob Taubes reminds us) clearly the apocalyptic thinker of counter-revolution: thus, an abyssal gulf opens up at the greatest proximity of these two political theologies. The realm of actuality is pregnant with potential eschatological breakthrough: this eschatological vision of history makes both Kierkegaard and Schmitt thinkers of transcendence who have turned against all illusions of immanence that has become 'normative' in the contemporary age of passionlessness and intensity. As thinkers of transcendence, they are both political theologians of 'authority'. This proximity, however, is also an irreducible distance: while Schmitt's political theology, in a counter-revolutionary manner, seeks to legitimate the figure of sovereignty as the true figure of *auctoritus* (thereby appealing to the theological

– 'Catholic' – foundation for its legitimation), Kierkegaard seeks delegitimation of all figures of *auctoritus* on the worldly order of *nomos* in the name of divine *auctoritus* that rules, not by *potestas* but by *agape*, the true heirs of this eschatological regime being not the sovereigns of the state and the Church but the martyrs and the apostles. In this profound sense, in the Kierkegaardian eschatological vision of political theology, Schmitt's transcendence will still be considered as immanence; or, at worst, it is a false transcendence. Schmitt's decisionism does not know the true exception, for the true exception must always, eternally, be exception, and, as such, it is truly *eschaton*: that what is always 'to come'. It does not become rule in turn. Schmitt's political theological attempt to restitute the authority of dictatorship in the worldly order is countered by a Kierkegaardian *kenotic* eschatology that denies any sovereign authority to any worldly institution in Christendom. For a Kierkegaardian *kenotic* eschatology, Schmittean political theology is grounded upon a mythic foundation (*arcanum*), as Schmitt himself explicitly acknowledges, which for Kierkegaard is a paganism or pantheism, just as with Hegel's immanent theodicy of history. At stake is the very sense of 'religion' which Kierkegaard rigorously distinguishes from all possible mythic foundation of worldly authorities.

Kierkegaard's reflection on the question of authority is most rigorously presented in his treatise 'Of the Difference between a Genius and an Apostle' (Kierkegaard 2010a). He begins with the qualitative difference between the genius and the Apostle: 'a genius and an Apostle are qualitatively different, they are definitions which each belong in their own spheres: *the sphere of immanence, and the sphere of transcendence*' (ibid.: 67; Kierkegaard's italics). Both the genius and the Apostle bring something new, but there is a qualitative difference between the new of the genius and the new of the Apostle: the new that the genius brings is assimilated over the years into the history of the race, while on the other hand, the new that the Apostle brings is paradoxically and eternally new, always already unassimilable to the human race, something qualitatively heterogeneous to the world-historical becoming, 'just as an Apostle remains an Apostle in all eternity' (ibid.). Belonging completely to the order of immanence, being what it is of itself, the genius 'has only an immanent teleology', while the Apostle 'is placed as absolute paradoxical teleology', being 'essentially, paradoxically different'. 'An Apostle is what he is by his divine authority' (ibid.: 67–8). What, then, is authority?

> Authority is, on the contrary, something which remained unchanged, which one cannot acquire even by understanding the doctrine perfectly. Authority is a specific quality which, coming from elsewhere, becomes qualitatively apparent when the content of the message or of the action is posited as indifferent. (Ibid.: 74)

If this is what authority is, 'coming from elsewhere', then it must be 'inconceivable within the sphere of immanence, or else it can only be thought of as something transitory' (ibid.: 75).

> Between God and man, then, there is and remains an eternal, essential, qualitative difference. *The paradox-religious relationship* (which, quite rightly, cannot be thought, but only believed) *appears when God appoints a particular man to divine authority*, in relation, be it carefully noted, to that which God has entrusted to him. The man thus called is no longer related as man to man qua man; his relationship to other man is not that of a qualitative difference (such as genius, exceptional gifts, position, etc.), he is related paradoxically by having a specific quality which no immanence can resolve in the equality of eternity; for it is essentially paradoxical and *after* that (not before, anterior to thought), contrary to thought. (Ibid.: 76–7; Kierkegaard's italics)

No human individual then (as man qua man), even though he is a genius, can claim sovereign authority on the basis of his own capacity and power. If there exists a semblance of 'authority' in the relation between man and man in the profane order of immanence, it can only be 'something transitory' which 'eternity does away with' (ibid.: 78). What 'eternity does away with' is 'worldly authority' which is 'physically recognizable by power', while the divine authority of the Apostle 'has no other proof than his own statement'; he is what 'he is through his paradoxical heterogeneity' (ibid.: 84). This is because, in respect to eternity, the whole worldly order of sovereignty is the order of transience which is *to* pass away, whose destiny is *to* pass away, and it is already passing away. This Kierkegaardian Pauline eschatology (for Paul too the order of the world is 'passing away') is very close to Benjaminian politics of nihilism: 'to strive after such passing, even for those stages of man that are nature, is the task of world politics, whose method must be called nihilism' (Benjamin 1986: 313).

As such, the true exception does not belong to the order of immanence, and it is not the prerogative of any worldly authority that rules by power in the realm of world-historical politics. The divine authority by its pure actuality of violence without the law (and therefore, it is a violence without violence) – which is the violence of the love – restitutes eternal life with the 'passing away' of the transient order. Therefore, suffering and mortification is the highest passion of religious life, for it alone opens us to life *as* life, life in its purity, and not the mere life upon which the violence of the law strikes as a fateful blow. Therefore, even Rosenzweig's great meditation on the meaning of redemption (which is so inspired by Schelling and Kierkegaard), just like Kierkegaard's, begins with the earnest contemplation of death and ends with life. This life, the redeemed life, is not the mere life under the ban of the law: it is where the human language, having come to its fulfilment, comes to its holy Sabbath. The true silence, both for Kierkegaard and Rosenzweig, is not the negation of speech; it is rather the fulfilment of speech; it is the Sabbath of speech. This fulfilled speech does away with all worldly 'chatter'. In the hegemonic order of the law, language has not yet reached its purity and beatitude; the concept, by its sheer cognitive violence, negates the messianic intensity of language that is constantly striving towards its redemption. That is why Kierkegaard could say that he who cannot be silent, cannot also speak essentially, and cannot speak the essential, for the essential – the one thing needful – has no other meaning than its very redemption, its Sabbath. Here our understanding stands still, having the 'web of reflection' done away with: this is the meaning of 'glory' which does not belong to the order of the world as it exists. Only by passing through the suffering on the cross, where God has *kenotically* emptied himself, can the new life and new understanding be gained: that the one who suffers humiliation is the very one who is, who will be, exulted. Kierkegaard contrasts the eschatological spirit of this New Testament Christianity – the new life (which, precisely, is the life of the Spirit) that takes birth by dying to the world – with Christendom that wilfully negates this 'gospel of suffering'. To understand this spirituality, which has nothing to do with the cosmism of paganism and Greek philosophy, it is necessary to undertake a 'self-examination' and a 'self-judgement', which means: to train oneself, each one for himself and herself, in utter solitude, to 'become sober':

> This life-giving in the Spirit is not a direct heightening of the natural life in a person in immediate continuation from and connection with it ... no, it is a new life, literally a new life – because, mark this well, death goes in between, dying to, and a life on the other side of death – yes, that is a new life. (Kierkegaard 1991: 76)

Conflagration

> I am come to send fire on the earth; and what will I, if it be already kindled?
> (Luke 12: 49)

The Pauline spirit of Kierkegaard's eschatology – that is: the Pauline disjunction between the cosmism of paganism and the *Pneuma* of Christianity, and Paul's understanding of the realm of nature as the order of 'passing away' – is much evident in Kierkegaard's two later texts, both written in polemical spirit (for what is Christianity if not polemical in its very essence?): *For Self-Examination* and *Judge For Yourself*. In these two texts, more explicitly than anywhere else, Kierkegaard's eschatology approaches the Pauline acosmic political theology: 'The middle ages' writes Kierkegaard in his journals, 'has been accused of acosmism – but in no case is cosmism Christianity. And yet the kind of culture and education supposedly identifiable with Christianity is almost the kind of culture that quite ingeniously is characterized by the phrase – to possess the world' (*JP* III 2712 (Pap. X3 A 588) N.D., 1850; see the 'Supplement' in Kierkegaard 1991: 256–7). The Christian dying to the world is, thus, the acosmism par excellence; it is the eschatological suspension of the law of nature:

> Death goes in between; this is what Christianity teaches, you must die to. The life-giving Spirit is the very one who slays you; the first thing the life-giving Spirit says is that you must enter into death, that you must die to – it is this way in order that you may not take Christianity in vain. A life-giving Spirit – that is the invitation; who would not willingly take hold of it! But die first – that is the halt! (Kierkegaard 1991: 76–7)

It is this 'dying to . . .' that introduces the abyssal breach with the world, and it is by virtue of this abyss that Christianity is absolutely heterogeneous to the world: 'abyssus abyssum invocat' (Ps. 42: 7). Christianity calls out to the abyss, invokes the abyss that eschatologically explodes the foundation of the world; the arrival of the unconditioned is the thunderstorm which is preceded by 'dialectics standing still':

> Before a thunderstorm there is sometimes such stillness, a still of a quite different kind; not a leaf stirs, not a breath of air. It is as if all nature stood still; nevertheless an almost imperceptible faint tremor goes through everything – what does the unconditioned stillness of this imperceptible tremor mean? It means that the unconditioned is expected, the thunderstorm. (Kierkegaard 1991: 108)

Kierkegaard himself expected this impending thunderstorm on the stage of history, and he also experienced it himself in the last years of his life: this is the way he lived the last years of his life, in imitation of Him who squandered his life, in his Passion, unto the cross. This *kenotic* Christ is 'divinely squanderous': 'if God in heaven were to clothe himself in the form of a humble servant, if he, divinely squanderous, if I dare put it this way, were to scatter around checks drawn upon heaven, human approval could not associate with greatness of that kind' (ibid.: 172). The divine *oikonomia* – which is non-economic par excellence (because it divinely squanders itself) – undoes all possible worldly economy ('human approval'): in this sense, 'dying to . . .' is profitless, useless dying, understood in accordance to the logic of the truth of the world. The truth of Christianity is not the worldly sagacity. According to Christianity, the worldly wisdom is intoxication, and idolatry against which Peter asks to 'become sober'. To become a Christian is to relinquish probability. The worldly sagacity feeds itself upon probability. To live christianly is to live life 'on the other side of probability'. 'In reliance upon God, venturing to relinquish probability is precisely what it means christianly to be sober' (ibid.: 103).

To live without probability – probability being the logic of worldly *oikonomia* – is to hope, against hope, for the un-hoped for ('the hope that is against hope' (ibid.: 83)): this strange hope, this mad hope – which, for Peter, paradoxically, is the only way to 'become sober' (against the hope for the hoped for, the latter hope being in accordance to natural understanding) – is the very offence of Christianity: the faith that the profitless dying of the Messiah on the cross, contra all economy, is to be redemptive for entire humanity and for the entire cosmos! Yet, this strange, abominable, offensive *oikonomia* beyond all economy is precisely the 'truth', the 'way', the 'life' of Christianity:

> that Christianity and being a true Christian must to the highest degree be an offense to the natural man, that he must regard Christianity as the greatest treason and the true Christian as the meanest traitor to being a human being, a treason and a traitor such as can never be punished severely enough. It is also easy to see that this is how Christianity, which is the qualification of the *Spirit*, must appear to anyone who has not, by dying to, been reborn to be *Spirit*. (Ibid.: 140)

Kierkegaard's political eschatology turns into a Pneumatology here: 'just like a straight line that touches the circle at only one point', the *Pneuma* is at once 'in the world and yet outside the world' (ibid.: 167). The (Kierkegaardian-Christian) *Pneuma*, unlike Hegelian phenomenology of spirit, does not end up, teleologically, in the harmony of the world, but comes to 'this collision with the world, with the human race, which the evil power incites, is also the history of the prototype' (ibid.: 170). The highest act of the true dialectics of spirit is, then, not that of 'reconciliation' and 'mediation' by the power of the cross (which is the very power of nothing, of non-actuality and of death), but to introduce the abyss of heterogeneity with the world 'by serving God alone' (ibid.: 169) who alone is Spirit par excellence. We can't recognise directly the glory of the Spirit: this is the whole illusion of immanence, and Hegel's dialectical theodicy of history is not immune from this dizzying illusion. What we need, then, is a new dialectic – the true dialectic of Spirit – of *kenosis* and glory:

> But just as the essentially Christian always places opposites together, so the glory is not directly known as glory but, just the reverse, is known by inferiority, debasement – the cross that belongs together with everything that is essentially Christian is here also . . . this is and always has been and will be an offense to the understanding. (Ibid.: 161)

'Pneuma' – Spirit – is, for Kierkegaard as much as for Paul, not the spirit of the world-history; it does not exult the world-historical movement into the figure of the absolute, for 'what is exulted among men is an abomination in the sight of God' (Luke 16: 15). *Pneuma* is not the *arché* – the hegemonic phantasm – of the world-historical domination; instead, by infinitely reminding us that Christianity is not 'the religion of mirth' but that of suffering, it undoes the *Koinon* that connects the worldly existence to its hegemonic phantasm: 'the religion of suffering has become the religion of mirth, but it retains the name unchanged' (Kierkegaard 1968: 142). One can imagine Kierkegaard writing his last great polemical essays holding the New Testament in his left hand, to show that 'Christendom' is a qualitatively different thing than Christianity.

In 1854 Bishop Mynster passed away. The Lutheran theologian Martensen, in his official eulogy, pronounced Bishop Mynster to be the true 'witness to the truth'. Kierkegaard was furious. He then embarked upon his last great attacks upon 'Christendom' (1854–5) in *Fatherland* – with the New Testament in left hand, accusing the 'silk and velvet priests' (ibid.: 35) in the biblical manner as 'serpents' and 'offspring of vipers'. Here is the biblical passage that inspired Kierkegaard's equally eschatological polemics, the passage that is seething in intensity with its eschatological judgements upon the 'silk and velvet priests':

> Woe unto you, scribes and Pharisees, hypocrites! For ye build the sepulchres of the prophets and garnish the tombs of the righteous, and say, if we had been in the days of our fathers, we should not have been partakers with them in the blood of the prophets. Wherefore yet witness to yourselves, that ye are sons of them that slew the prophets. Fill up then the measure of your fathers. Ye serpents, ye offspring of vipers, how shall ye escape the judgment of hell? (Matthew 23: 29–33)

Or, the same saying of Christ from Luke (11: 47–8):

> Woe unto you! For ye build the tombs of the prophets and your father killed them. So ye are witnesses and consent unto the works of your fathers; for they killed them, and ye build their tombs.

Kierkegaard here follows Christ's exhortation, thereby becoming 'contemporary' with him, but without 'authority', to 'beware of those who go about in long robes' (Mark 12: 38; Luke 20: 46). To be contemporary, that is, to be 'Christian' is 'to be a sacrifice, sacrificed on behalf of a generation for which ideals are nonsense, are naught, for which the earthly and the temporal are seriousness, a generation which worldly shrewdness in the form of Christian teachers has shamefully, in a Christian sense, demoralized' (Kierkegaard 1968: 65). 'To witness to the truth' is not to go about in 'long robes' and silk; to be Christian is not to conquer the world by world-political means, but by welcoming the fourth state where martyrs rule (that is, without 'ruling' by force and by power).

> A witness to the truth is a man who in poverty witnesses to the truth – in poverty, in lowliness, in abasement, and so is unappreciated, hated, abhorred, and then derided, insulted, mocked – his daily bread perhaps he did not always have, so poor was he, but the daily dose of persecution he was richly provided with everyday. (Ibid.: 7)

The term 'witness to the truth', then, implies undoing the worldly economy of symmetry and harmony; it means to introduce that element that makes Christianity 'heterogeneous to the world', 'by renunciation, by suffering' (ibid.: 11), for the arrival of the Messiah sets the world on fire 'to smoke out illusions and knavish tricks', which is

> a police raid, and a Christian police raid, for, according to the New Testament, Christianity is incendiarism, Christ Himself says, 'I am come to set fire on the earth', and it is already burning, yea, and it is doubtless becoming a consuming conflagration, best likened to a forest fire, for it is 'Christendom' that is set on fire. And it is the prolixities which have to go, the prodigiously prolix illusion fostered by the (well-meant or knavish) introduction of scientific learning into the Christian field, the prodigiously prolix conceit about millions of Christians, Christian kingdoms and lands, a whole world of Christians . . . the official Christianity is not the Christianity of the New Testament. (Ibid.: 41)

Against the secularised theodicy of Christendom, Kierkegaard seeks to renew the apocalyptic incendiarism of the New Testament. This acute apocalyptic intensity can be renewed only by reintroducing the unconditioned in the midst of history, 'like the spring of the wild beast, or like the swift blow of the bird of prey'. Such apocalyptic Christianity can only be militant and polemic Christianity which must supply the unconditioned as the very immeasurable measure of history, and thereby apply it as a 'corrective' on 1,800 years of Christendom. Such a 'corrective' cannot but be one-sided: it 'must study accurately and profoundly the weak side of the establishment, and then vigorously and one-sidedly present the opposite' (ibid.: 90), for 'only either/or is the embrace which grasps the unconditional' (ibid.: 82). The apocalyptic dialectic, as Kierkegaard's dialectic aspires itself to be, is the dialectic of 'either/or' 'which grasps the unconditional'; it nourishes itself upon the abyss of disproportion – the 70,000 fathoms of depth – that 'smokes out' all illusions of proportion and harmony.

> The state is inversely proportionate to number (the numerical); therefore, when a state is decreasing its numbers may gradually become so small that the state ceases to exist, the concept is snuffed out.

> Christianity stands in a different relation to number; one single true Christian is enough to justify the assertion that Christianity exists. In fact, Christianity is inversely proportionate to number; for the concept 'Christian' is a polemical concept, one can only be a Christian in contrast or contrastedly. So it is also in the New Testament: to God's desire to be loved, which essentially is a relationship of contrast or opposition in order to raise love to a higher power, corresponds the fact that the Christian who loves God in contrast and opposition to other men has to suffer from their hate and persecution. As soon as the opposition is taken away, the thing of being a Christian is twaddle – as it is in 'Christendom' which has slyly done away with Christianity by the affirmation that we are all Christians. (Ibid.: 127)

Therefore, we must make the qualitative disjunction between the two:

> it is necessary to practise separation, discrimination, between the infinite and the finite, between a striving for the infinite and the finite, between living for something and living by something, which our age – most indecently! – has put together in the closet, got them to curdle together or coalesce into one, which Christianity on the contrary, with the passion of eternity, with the most dreadful either/or, holds apart from one another, separating them by a yawning abyss. (Ibid.: 144)

This opposition cannot be equated with any (Schmittean) theologico-political opposition of friend/enemy; for the apocalyptic dialectic of Kierkegaard's political theology *unworks* in advance any such (Schmittean) opposition by introducing, at the heart of symmetrical opposition, an unheard opposition of absolute heterogeneity. Loving God, for Kierkegaard, is to love the enemy; it is not the 'syrupy sweets in which falsehood's witnesses to the truth are wont to deal':

> How dreadful (speaking merely in a human way) is God in His love, so dreadful it is (speaking merely in human way) to be loved of God and to love God. In the declaration that God is love, the subordinate clause is, He is thy mortal enemy. (Ibid.: 158)

One must practise 'setting apart', but this apocalyptic political theology is no Schmittean political theology of 'friend' set apart from 'the enemy'. The Catholic Schmitt's *analogia entis* meets here the Lutheran *destructio* of all analogia:

> A Christian ought to be if possible His majesty's best subject. But christianly, the king is not the prerogative authority, he is and can and must and will not be the prerogative authority in relation to a Kingdom which is not willing at any price to be of this world, come life, come death, will not be of this world. (Ibid.: 103)

This is the Lutheran-Kierkegaardian eschatological reading: 'Render therefore unto Caesar the things which are Caesar's; and unto God the things that are God's' (Matthew 22: 21). This is taken in the sense of the eschatological reserve and withdrawal of the ultimate normative obligation to any worldly power 'inasmuch as Christianity is the antithesis to the Kingdoms of this world, is heterogeneous, not to be royally authorized is the truer thing' (Kierkegaard 1968: 133). Therefore, the state is not justified in receiving an oath from the teachers of Christianity. 'Such an oath is self-contradiction, like making a man swear by laying his hand upon the New Testament, where it is written, Thou shalt not swear' (ibid.: 130).

> The Christian demand upon the state must be to the following effect: whether the State, the sooner the better, might not be so good as to dispense all the clergy from their oath upon the New Testament, gave them back the oath, as an expression of the fact that the State has got into something it cannot meddle with, which at the same time will express what is true, that God, if I may venture to say so, discharges the whole actual garrison of priests, gives them back their oath. (Ibid.: 131)

The similarity of Nietzschean diagnosis with Kierkegaardian deconstruction of 'Christendom' is again seen here: 1,800-year-old Christendom has become a tranquiliser and a sedative, while Christianity 'is in the deepest sense arousing, disquieting' (ibid.: 262); there has occurred a 'reversal' of the ideal: the exception is replaced with slave mentality where mediocre ones honour each other: 'how can ye believe who receive honor from one another?' (John 5: 44). 'To receive honor from one another' – 'the witness to the truth' – is the symptom that it is not Christianity but Christendom that is at place: such a witness is like a commandant who build bridges for enemy to take the fortress of Christianity who transforms the fortress into the countryseat of Christendom (Kierkegaard 1968: 138). This 'apostasy' – from the fortress into the countryseat – has the commandant (Bishop Mynster or Bishop Martensen) who 'slyly, cunningly, knavishly, by everybody assuming the name of being Christian', has invented 'a sweetmeat which has a delicious taste, for which men hand out their money with delight' (ibid.: 46–7). The salvation has thus become a commodity in the marketplace of the world-historical politics; the apocalyptic and anti-nomic world-denial characteristic of Christianity (which demands 'a total transformation in a man, to wrest from him through renunciation and self-denial all that, and precisely that, to which he immediately clings, in which he immediately has his life' (ibid.: 221)) has been transformed into the countryseat of mirth where velvet priests in long robes go about, honouring each other with 'witness to the truth'. What is, then, taken away is the wound that Christianity introduced 'on the most dreadful scale' possible that collides with everything in the world:

> In the New Testament, Christianity is the profoundest wound that can be inflicted upon a man, calculated on the most dreadful scale to collide with everything – and now the clergyman has perfected himself in introducing Christianity in such a way that it signifies nothing, and when he is able to do this to perfection he is regarded as a paradigm. (Ibid.: 258)

Bishop Mynster and Bishop Martensen have, thus, become 'paradigms' of Christianity who applause every time the Church comes to work in harmony with the state. Christianity no longer pounds 'the table hard in front of us men', because everyone is today Christian in Christendom; there is no more 'dissension' which Christ introduced once – 'that of the "individual" with the "race", with the millions, with family, with father and mother' (ibid.: 166). Instead, there has occurred successful dialectical mediation of all opposites, dissensions and collisions:

> If two men were to eat nuts together, and the one liked only the shell, the other only the kernel, one may say that they match one another well. What the world rejects, casts away, despises, namely the sacrificed man, the kernel – precisely upon that God sets the greatest store, and treasures it with greater zeal than does the world that which it loves with the greatest passion. (Ibid.: 198)

The sub-text here is the passage on beatitude (Matthew 5: 3–11): here is the Kierkegaardian eschatological vision of beatitude. The messianic kingdom belongs to the sacrificed – kenotic – ones: this cannot be understood as another, albeit higher, instance of earthly *oikonomia*. Rigorously thought, this negates any economy of self-presence: nothing is guaranteed, no profit is anticipatable and no return is insured. Beatitude is not something that is earned, by any work or merit; as pure gratuitous gift, it calls for costly discipleship, 'for here in the world truth walks in lowliness and humiliation, has not where to lay its head, must be thankful if one will give it a cup of water' (Kierkegaard 1968: 249). Beatitude is rather the eschatological 'breaking through of the eternal' (ibid.: 281) at the Instant: 'the Instant is when *the* man is there, the right man, the man of the Instant' (ibid.: 280). But this Instant – this is the very last, and also the very first thought of Kierkegaard – does not belong to any immanence of self-presence; it is the qualitative disjunction, or epochal breakthrough which eternity enters as this Instant, and no other, as the point degree zero of history.

> Things may go on for hundreds of thousands and millions of years constantly the same – it looks perhaps as if it might now soon come; but so long as there is only worldly shrewdness and mediocrity, etc., the Instant comes not, no more than does an unfruitful man beget children. (Ibid.: 281)

If one marches along with the Hegelian Spirit, the Instant will never come. The Hegelian theodicy of history is like 'an unfruitful man': one may march on and on, for millions of years, the Instant may not come. The 1,800 years of Christendom proving itself to be victorious at the level of world-historical politics, does not prove the truth of Christianity, and the attempt to prove it by historical reason transforms the eternal truth of Christianity into a hypothesis. In that sense, the time of world-history remains a homogenous and empty time, as Walter Benjamin remarks, for it knows not the Instant: Benjamin comes to call it *Nunc Stans* when 'dialectics comes to a standstill'. The Instant is the 'breaking through of the eternal' (ibid.): this – this 'fact that the eternal once came into existence in time' – 'is not something which has to be tested in time, not something which *men are to test*, but is the paradox by which *men are to be tested* (Kierkegaard 1994: 160–1). Instead of participating in the triumphal march of the Hegelian theodicy of history, it passes judgement upon the violence of the historical reason. It is because the Hegelian Spirit does not follow 'the way', which is not the way of intensification of harmony but the messianic intensification of difference, between the truth and truths, between the truth and truths of the world. It is the narrow and strained way – the way of the cross – that 'leadeth unto life, and few are they that find it' (Matthew 7: 14). This life here is not bare life under the force of the law, but the beatific life of glory that has passed through the unbearable agony of *kenosis*. This is the object of faith that demands sacrifice, and not the *figuration* of the Absolute Knowledge that knows not the essential crucifixion of the divine-human life. Lacking the ethical element which undergoing the abyss of crucifixion alone gives us, the *figuration* of the Absolute Knowledge lacks one thing: the unconditioned itself. Kierkegaard's political theology has this sole consideration, this one thing necessary: the infinite, non-negotiable demand of the unconditional that alone makes us, as St Peter says, completely 'sober'. Nothing is more monstrous than the human who exists without this infinite demand that comes as the breakthrough of the eternal. Kierkegaard hears the infinite verbality of this unconditioned in the New Testament Christianity which he, with his vehement passion, sets apart from the Christendom of mirth and vulgar celebration of worldly economy that has become this very world.

Notes

1. 'Christianly understood, the truth consists not in knowing the truth but in being the truth' (Kierkegaard 2004: 184); truth is 'a being, a life' (ibid.: 185); 'truth as a form of being' (ibid.): existence!
2. Christ's form on earth as a servant means un-recognisability: 'to be the individual man, or an individual man (whether it be a distinguished or a lowly man is here irrelevant), is the greatest possible, the infinitely qualitative, remove from being God, and therefore the profoundest incognito' (Kierkegaard 2004: 112). And: 'the unrecognizableness of

the God-Man is an incognito almightily maintained, and the divine seriousness consists precisely in the fact that it is so almightily maintained that He himself suffers under His unrecognizableness in a purely human way' (ibid.: 116).
3. 'The divine compassion, its limitless *abandon* in its concern for the sufferer alone – not in the least for itself – and the absolute *abandon* with which it concerns itself for *every* sufferer – that cannot but be interpreted by men as a sort of insanity, which one hardly knows whether to laugh or to weep over' (Kierkegaard 2004: 53; Kierkegaard's italics).
4. 'That the human race is or should be akin to God is ancient paganism; but that an individual man is God is Christianity . . . As such it reveals itself in the situation of contemporaneousness; and no relationship with God-Man is possible except by beginning with the situation of contemporaneousness' (Kierkegaard 2004: 69–70).
5. Karl Löwith writes: 'Thus in spite of his polemic against Hegel's process, the force of the age led even Kierkegaard to historical speculation and, against Marx, to an anticommunist manifesto. He went so far as to predict the danger which would come when the catastrophe broke: false prophets of Christianity will then arise, inventors of a new religion, who, infected with demons, will arrogantly declare themselves apostles, like thieves in the costume of police. Thanks to their promise, they will receive terrible support from the age, until it finally becomes clear that the age stands in need of the absolute, and a restoration of Christendom through martyr-witnesses who allow themselves to be slain for the truth, Kierkegaard is the contemporary antithesis to Marx's propaganda of a proletarian world revolution. As the actual strength of Communism, Kierkegaard saw the "ingredient" of Christian religiosity which it still contained' (Löwith 1991: 114).
6. Thus Schmitt writes: 'To the conceptions of God in the seventeenth and eighteenth centuries belongs the idea of his transcendence vis-à-vis the world, just as to the period's philosophy of state belongs the notion of the transcendence of the sovereign vis-à-vis the state. Everything in the nineteenth century was increasingly governed by conceptions of immanence. All the identities that recur in the political ideas and in the state doctrines of the nineteenth century rest on such conceptions of immanence: the democratic thesis of the identity of the rule and the ruled, the organic theory of the state with the identity of the state and sovereignty . . .' (Schmitt 2005: 49–50). Schmitt, then, goes on to write: 'Conceptions of transcendence will no longer be credible to most educated people, who will settle for either a more or less clear immanence-pantheism or a positivist indifference toward any metaphysics. Insofar as it retains the concept of God, the immanence philosophy, which found its greatest systematic architect in Hegel, draws God into the world and permits law and the state to emanate from the immanence of the objective' (ibid.: 50).

Chapter 4

Sovereign Love

> Beloved, let us love one another: for love is of God; and every one that loveth is born of God, and knoweth God. (1 John 4: 7)

Love without sovereignty

This chapter takes Kierkegaard's book *Works of Love* to show – against the dominant understanding of his work – that the question of sociality lies at the very heart of Kierkegaard's political theology. While Kierkegaard is often portrayed as the solitary – even solipsistic – thinker of the 'single individual' as against the totalising claims of the crowd and the mass, a careful and rigorous study of his direct discourses, above all his *Works of Love*, discloses the other side of his polemical negative dialectic. Here we are exposed – through self-examination and judging each one for him-/herself – to the thorn of the second commandment: 'love your neighbour as you love yourself': here all erotic self-love is wounded and exposed to the radical alterity of the neighbour. We can call such an ethics as *indicative ethics* whose decisive constituent element is, to begin and to end with, love alone. The abyss of love is irreducible to the sovereign attributes of the law and to the power of its judgement. In this paradoxical way – Kierkegaard appears to be saying this without saying it in such explicit terms – love alone is sovereign, divinely sovereign, in that it alone is without sovereignty. In this sense too Kierkegaard remains closer to Schelling's political theology of love than to Hegel's theodicy of Absolute Knowledge.

In *Works of Love* Kierkegaard constructs elements of an *indicative ethics* which surpasses politics like an infinite surplus which, in turn, effectively throws into question the totalising claims of politics. Instead of Hegel's speculative-dialectical reconciliation of love with knowledge, here we find a negative theological insistence on the radical invisibility of love that infinitely surpasses the light of knowledge, even that of Hegelian Absolute Knowledge. One that reminds us of Pseudo-Dionysius's negative theology of 'dazzling darkness', for Kierkegaard the light of love grows dazzlingly dark when one approaches it with the force of the concept, with the violence of the law, with the attributes of judgement.

Such an indicative ethics of love, inspired by Johannine sociality of Christian neighbour-love, makes Kierkegaard's political theology an effective foil against the political theology of Carl Schmitt who makes politics total. The law of love, where the 'law' is understood as 'commandment' – the second commandment 'love thy neighbour' – is irreducible to the instituted truth of the juridico-political realm: this insight, that love is irreducible to judgement, is the decisive teaching of Kierkegaard's *direct* communication. It is possible to say that it is towards this 'dazzling darkness' of love that Kierkegaard's *direct* communication receives its *direction*. The result here is a political theology of love without sovereignty, and for that matter, paradoxically, it is a political theology of sovereign love.

The Johannine sociality of love

That Kierkegaard is a solitary thinker – who in his work addresses that 'single individual' called 'the reader' – is no doubt a 'correct' interpretation of Kierkegaard, the interpretation that can be substantiated with lot of citations from Kierkegaard's own works. However, it has often been taken to mean that Kierkegaard thereby refuses any ethical idea of 'being-with' (sociality or community) as totalitarian: this interpretation needs re-evaluation. It still needs to be shown that the Kierkegaardian negative dialectical either/or is not so much either/or between the solitary individual, enclosed in his/her solipsist self, and the totalitarian claims of any sociality (which Kierkegaard calls 'the crowd'). And it still needs to be shown that at the heart of Kierkegaardian thought of Christianity lies the idea of a messianic-eschatological sociality to come where 'being-with' is nourished by the singularity of the 'becoming-a-self'. For, to interrupt, to disrupt or to break any worldly hegemony (Kierkegaard calls it 'Christendom' which is a qualitatively different thing from Christianity), it is not enough to insist on the single individual alone, as if singularity is an enclosed totality antithetically opposed to the other totality called 'the universal'. 'To emphasise 'the singular individual' is not a refusal of 'being-with'. Kierkegaard does not remain content with the simple opposition to the order of totality by 'the single individual' who is enclosed in one's self; and he does not thereby merely replace the 'maximizing thrust' (Schürmann 2003) of the universal. For, to merely oppose a totality ('the single individual') against another totality ('the universal') reduplicates the very phantasm that founds any hegemonic regime in the first place. Such a gesture or strategy of 'replacement' or antithesis reduplicates the 'tragic denial' that gives rise to the hegemonies.

The task, therefore, should be conceived as interruption of any totality at all. The 'being-with' then, as Kierkegaard understands it, is not to be confused with any 'empirical' totality, given to us as the 'natural' entity constituted by blood ties, or by being tied to the political regimes at place through normative obligations. In this sense, despite Kierkegaard's adamant protest against contemporary Protestantism, Kierkegaard remains 'Protestant' in spirit, if not in letter. Protesting against all *aesthetisation* of theology (that is, glorification of the natural order), Kierkegaard retains the rigour of either/or. The world of nature, as Pauline theology insists, is 'to pass away'. To deify this order of transiency whose destiny is to pass away is precisely what the hegemonic regime of Christendom has accomplished. To reintroduce Christianity into Christendom, after 1,800 years, is to gladly let *pass away* what is *to* pass away. It is in this eschatological light (where all that is nature is thought to be provisional and transient) that Kierkegaard's 'deconstruction' of totality – especially Hegelian metaphysics of universal history – is to be understood. Such 'deconstruction' of totality (which claims itself universality) demands a true 'being-with', released from normative obligation to a community of blood ties or to the political regime at place; it affirms a 'being-with' – a community without *Koinon* – that interrupts any mythic fusion (where this mythic fusion operates as the very principle of fascism). Irreducible to any given, empirically available and already constituted 'community', it is the eschatological *sociality to come*. In the very Johannine sense, it can be called *sociality of love*: 'Beloved, let us love one another: for love is of God; and every one that loveth is born of God, and knoweth God' (1 John 4: 7).

Søren Kierkegaard's *Works of Love* is perhaps the most Johannine-Kierkegaardian text par excellence, for this immense work can be understood as a profound commentary on John's loving and gentle exhortation to love, the softening of the commandment to love one's neighbour: 'Thou shalt love thy neighbour as thyself.' What is an imperative, in all the rigour of its commandment, becomes in John a gentle exhortation: 'Beloved, let us love one another: for love is of God; and every one that loveth is born of God, and knoweth God.' The messianic sociality of love – love that does not rule by the force of law, but by the commandment that demands that humanity renounces force – is a radically 'new' community which is to be constantly renewed by 'works of love'. The universal world-order that

Kierkegaard vehemently attacks – the homogenisation of people, the massification of people into 'crowd' and so-called 'democracy' (the political regime ruled by the phantasm called 'the public') – is the order of totality whose constitutive principle is a sovereign phantasm. To think outside such an order of totality demands that the irreducible element of singularity must be thought as the very fecund principle of 'being-with', of a messianic sociality. What other than *love* can give us that singular 'being-with' (which makes possible to think singularity itself in a new and irreducible way)? This singularity is irreducible to be a mere particular instantiation of the universal; it is also thereby not an enclosed totality, a solipsistic self, another universal in turn.

That is why the interpretation that Kierkegaard violently asserts a virile subjectivity of protest and thereby nullifies any ethical relation of responsibility to the other(s); in fact, the understanding that he nullifies anything 'ethical' at all, since for Kierkegaard the 'religious' stage rules supreme – such an interpretation (Lévinas 1998: 26–38) needs serious re-evaluation. *Works of Love* shows, on the contrary, that one's opening to the other – the neighbour, the neighbour who is the first to come by – is already commanded by Christian love in an irreducible way, which is possible because the love of God – the first commandment – has *always already* torn the subjectivity open, exposed, and responsible to the other. In that sense, the originality and irreducibility of the second commandment of love is *always already* implied in the first commandment: to show this is precisely the task that Kierkegaard undertakes in *Works of Love*.

Kierkegaard, however, already anticipated the misunderstanding that he knew no ethical idea of sociality. Here is an entry to his *Journal* at the time of writing *Works of Love*:

> In spite of everything men ought to have learned about my maieutic carefulness, in addition to proceeding slowly and continually letting it seem as if I knew nothing more, not the next thing – now on the occasion of my new Edifying Discourses they will presumably bowl out that I don't know what comes next, that I knew nothing about sociality. The fools! Yet on the other hand I owe it to myself to confess before God that in a certain sense there is something truth in it, only not as men understand it, namely that always when I have first presented one aspect sharply and clearly, then I affirm the validity of the other even more strongly. Now I have the theme of the next book. It will be called *Works of Love*. (*Journals or Papirer* VIII A4; quoted by the translator in Kierkegaard 1964: 17–18)

It is the idiomatic and singular 'strategy' or 'style' of Kierkegaardian thinking (which is not a 'method' that can be mechanically applied) that the presentation of 'the single individual', as against the pan-logical totality of concepts ('system', namely the Hegelian system that denies the singularity of existence), demands that the element of singularity is to be emphasised 'sharply and clearly' in his field of *polemos*. This misleads the reader to think that Kierkegaard has no ethical consciousness of sociality. This misreading conveniently ignores the other side of Kierkegaardian *polemos*, the other side of the qualitative dialectic: that 'when I have first presented one aspect sharply and clearly, then I affirm the validity of the other even more strongly'. The very 'dialectical' nature of Kierkegaardian *polemos* demands that the problematic of sociality may be presented even more strongly. We should be able to perceive here the double-edged sword of Kierkegaardian deconstruction; not only that what Kierkegaard means by 'the single individual' is not how it is taken to be meant (the closed, private, solipsistic self), but also that what Kierkegaard means by 'sociality' is also not to be taken in the more obvious, given and prevalent sense of the term: the radically new idea of 'subjectivity' – or 'self' – demands, at the same movement of thinking, a radically new idea of 'sociality'. The solitude of subjectivity ('that single individual') must be read, once again, after it has been strongly emphasised (against the subjectivity of Hegelian logical metaphysics) – this is the dialectical double reading – in the new light of sociality. Thus, sociality is not a mere accidental appendix to the fundamental principle of 'the single individual' in Kierkegaardian *polemos*. In the same manner, in the Kierkegaardian interpretation, the second commandment of love is not a mere accidental appendix to the first commandment of love. The one necessarily follows the other: the love of God demands that the human loves his or her neighbour in the light of the love of God, making Love itself the witness that exceeds them, if love is not to degenerate into the selfish love of the solipsistic self. Thus, in the manner that we should be able to distinguish between love and love, between the neighbour-love that is commanded and the aesthetised erotic love of the closed self, so must we be able to distinguish between self and self, between the singular subjectivity exposed open from all closure by Love, and the natural self that is given as a private individual, which does not need to 'become' in love.

The singular self, then, is never given as a natural entity, a biological something, a number in a state-sponsored census report; it is neither a shadowy appearance in the public opinion as expressed by the overwhelmingly powerful media (the press is Kierkegaard's example), nor is it a vote, a carrier of an identity mark in a 'democratic' system of government where everyone fantasises oneself as a ruler. The singular self – and this is what 'existence' means for Kierkegaard – is rather 'becoming': the-ecstatic-*coming*-into-the-open, out of all closures, the self who is called by love to be open to the wholly Other Love. Only such a singular self can be truly social – and thus, can truly be *self* – where sociality is no longer understood as natural something. Sociality, in its true sense, cannot be thought of as something like a political organisation joined together by mutual self-interests, as if a mere multiplicity and mutuality of many self-interests coming together can be called 'social'. It is rather qualitatively, and in an infinite sense – like the singular self – is a *new* becoming, the-ecstatic-*coming*-into-the-open in the neighbour-love. The neighbour-love, then, truly demands a *breaking* of the (selfish) self – self that does not *become*; similarly, it also demands a *breaking* of the prevalent idea of the neighbour itself, the neighbour as the natural determinant (as empirically given, the neighbour who is next to my territory, whether this territory is understood geographically, linguistically, racially or even metaphysically). What breaks the neighbour as the natural determinant, and what breaks the self, which is a natural determinant, is the commandment *as* commandment that functions not as the force of the law but as the exhortation of love. Therefore, Kierkegaard's idea of sociality is not so much concerned with love, but with *works* of love. In this fulfilment of the commandment that love acts, and which indeed is the *work* of love, the force of law itself (the law enacted by the state, or by any anonymous order of instituted totality) is undone. Love gives birth, eschatologically, to a *new* self and a *new* sociality: this is the *work* of love, that is, to give birth; it presupposes death of the old self (as natural determinant) and of the old community (as the political regime at place, as natural determinant). Such birth, passing through death and mortification, is of resurrected self, and of a new sociality that the Johannine Gospel orients us towards: 'let us love one another'.

In his *polemos* against the tyrannical order of generality ('crowd'), against the violence of history, Kierkegaard indeed insists on the single individual in the light of the Lutheran *theologia crucis*; however, the other moment – the glory of God, namely, the resurrection – is not forgotten; it remains as the eschatological moment for Kierkegaard's thought as the very Johannine sociality of love. To take up one moment exclusively – the cross without the glory – as Kierkegaardian, is to not properly understand the double reading that Kierkegaard himself enacts in his *polemos*. When one takes up the double moments in Kierkegaardian thought – in their very irreducible *polemos* – then the affirmative character of Kierkegaard's deconstruction becomes manifest: that Kierkegaard indeed is the thinker of affirmation par excellence, an affirmation that must pass through the crucifixion of self-examination or judging oneself. The cross judges by its very suffering; it judges *each* one of us absolutely singularly, and it judges *me* above and before everyone. However, this judgement is not the judgement of the law by its force, but a judgement of love that suffers on the cross. In this strict sense, the judgement of the cross is no 'judgement', for where there is love, there is no judgement (of the law). The cross has put to death all judgement of the law; now what remains, at the end, is only the Johannine exhortation: 'let us love one another'. This judgement of love, if it is to be called 'judgement' still, frees us rather than imprisons us in the prison house of the law, and yet it binds us at the same time – binding without the violence of force and without the gaze of the law – to the duty without measure, a duty that exceeds even the bounds of mere reason, duty that goes beyond all regulative principles of practical reason. It is to such duty that Kierkegaard exhorts us in this Johannine text *Works of Love*. How can love – where love, by definition, is free – be yet dutiful, for all duty binds us? Is there a specific duty or task of love that frees us and yet binds us, frees us by binding us, binds us by freeing us, at the same time – which would truly be called *work of love* – a duty which exceeds the duty that the regulative principle of reason evokes?

How can there be duty to love? Such duty, if it is indeed the 'work of love' as Kierkegaard calls it, cannot be understood in terms of the regulative principle of reason. Without naming Kant here, Kierkegaard puts into question the Kantian 'religion of reason within the bounds of mere reason'. Only such duty of love, exceeding the bounds of mere reason, can truly think of a free, messianic sociality where the freedom is dutiful, in the name of love, and in the name Love that dies on the cross. Only a free self – free in love, and therefore truly *self* – is free for a free sociality. Kierkegaard's qualitative dialectics attends to this double reading, and it is important for us to attend to these double moments, in their very heterogeneity: the cross and the glory, the singular self and the eschatological sociality of love, duty and freedom – summed up, in this Johannine exhortation: 'let us love one another':

> We shall now conclude by introducing John the apostle, saying: "Behold, let us love one another". These words, which consequently have apostolic authority, also have, if you will consider them, a middle tone or a middle mood with respect to the contrasts in love itself, which has its basis in that they are said by one perfected in love. You don't hear in these words the rigorousness of duty; the apostle does not say: 'You *shall* love one another'; but neither do you hear the intensity of inclination, of poet passion. There is something transfigured and blessed in these words, but also a sadness which broods over life and is tempered by the eternal. It is as if the apostle said, 'Dear me, what is all this which would hinder you from loving; what is all this which you can win by self-love: the commandment is that you *shall* love, but when you understand life and yourself, then it is as if you should not need to be commanded, because to love human beings is the only the thing worth living for; without this love you really do not really live; to love human beings is also the only salutary consolation for both time and eternity, and to love human beings is the only true sign that you are a Christian' – truly a profession of faith is not enough. Christianly understood, love is commanded; but the commandment of love is the old

commandment, which is always new. It is not with the love-commandment as with a human command, which becomes old with the years or is changed by the mutual agreement of those who should obey it. No, the love-commandment remains new until the last day, just as new even on the last day when it has become most ancient. Consequently the commandment is not altered in the slightest way, least of all by an apostle. The only change can be, then, that the lover becomes more and more intimate with the commandment, becomes more and more one with the commandment, which he loves: therefore he is able to speak so mildly, so sadly, almost as if it has been forgotten that love is the commandment. If, however, you forget that it is the apostle of love who speaks, then you misunderstand him, for such words are not the beginning of the discourse on love but are the consummation of love. Therefore we don't dare talk this way. That which is truth in the mouth of veteran, perfected apostle could in the mouth of a beginner easily be flirtation, whereby he would seek to leave and commandment's school much too soon and escape the *school-yoke*. We introduce the apostle speaking; we do not make his words into our own but make ourselves into hearers of 'Beloved, let us love one another'. (*Journals or Papirer* VIII A4; quoted by the translator in Kierkegaard 1964: 16–17)

Kierkegaard's *wink*: an indicative ethics

Is it possible to conceive of a Kierkegaardian ethics? In an obvious sense, the answer appears to be 'no'.

1. Kierkegaard's solitary subjectivity, persecuted in its truth and withdrawn from the visibility of universal history, is a virile subjectivity; wrapped up in its closure, it shuts its door against the other who is every bit other, for the subjectivity, in its jealous insistence on its singularity and on its irreducible secret, is afraid that its singularity will be lost if it has to give up its closure. Hence is its virile *polemos* against all forms of visibility as necessarily violent; the result, paradoxically, is its own violence against the visible, the general and the anonymous order of totality. This is something like a Lévinasian reading of Kierkegaard.
2. Kierkegaard's own understanding of the ethical as one of the stages of life – and not the highest – makes it difficult to think of the fundamental attunement of his thinking as such as ethical. The ethical occurs, in Kierkegaardian stages of life, as the mediated stage to which the aesthetic immediacy has to pass itself over. In this sense, Kierkegaard would say, Hegel is indeed right: the dark night of the particular in its idiosyncrasy and sensuous immediacy cannot maintain its abstract particularity against the claim of the visible, of the universal and of the communicable. If this is what the ethical is – a stage of life, in-

between (not in the temporal-successive sense) the not-yet ethical (the aesthetic immediacy) and surpassing-the-ethical (the religious) – then Kierkegaard's thinking cannot be called *ethical* as the fundamental attunement of his thinking *as such*.

In what sense then can we say that the ethical is the fundamental attunement of his thinking as such? It can be understood neither in the dialectical sense of Hegel's speculative-historical thought where the *telos* is the Absolute Knowledge that, as it were, threatens to swallow up the singular subjectivity by the integrative-subsuming violence of the concept, nor can it be understood in terms of the Kantian regulative principle of reason which supplies only the universal maxims, and which does not address 'me' as *me* in my absolute singularity of existence. It cannot be understood as prescriptive-normative ethics, in which case the unconditional disappears (for the unconditional love or justice cannot be reduced to prescribed and normative); it also cannot be understood as merely regulative in order to preserve the unconditional, for then the unconditional becomes a mere shadow, an empty promise of homogenous and vacant eternity, an endless task over a very long time that addresses humanity *as such* but not *me* in *fear and trembling*, impatient in suffering, confronting that absolute Other who is wholly other in faith.

Such an ethical task which unconditionally addresses the singular being (not the aesthetic, immediate, sensuous, particular being: he is already exposed open by the visible *work* of history) with its singular, existential task of faith, absolved from the totalising universality of genus or species, such an ethical task can only be *indicative*. Such is the Kierkegaardian *wink*: the ethical, as it were, has to occur at the limit of knowledge, even that of Absolute Knowledge; a peril of knowledge, madness it is, as it were. The unconditional neutralises its eschatological intensity if it were seen merely as a task of humanity over its very long time of world-historical politics. The *wink* indicates beyond what is presently available, over and beyond what is presently visible in the world, beyond what constitutes the world as 'the world', the world as the space of the visible; the *wink* indicates the radical invisible origin – of what Kierkegaard would call 'eternity' which each time is irreducible to fleeting instances of worldly time of profane history – that radically invisible source from which the commandment is issued forth: you *shall* love. Such unconditional may be heard and affirmed only by an absolute faith of love at the limit of knowledge; it introduces a tear in the veil of the visible. The invisibility of love that the *wink* indicates is not a mere attenuated variation of the visible; rather it indicates, at the heart of the visible, the wholly other, the radical *absconditus* that does not belong to profane history.

Therefore, *Works of Love* begins with the invocation of the invisible, and *invocation* it is which the very language of *indication* is:

> The hidden life of love is in the most inward depths, unfathomable, and still has an unfathomable relationship with the whole of existence. As the quiet lake is fed deep down by the flow of hidden springs, which no eye sees, so a human being's love is grounded, still more deeply, in God's love. If there were no spring at the bottom, if God were not love, then there would be neither a little lake nor a man's love. As the still water begins obscurely in the deep spring, so a man's love mysteriously begins in God's love. As the quiet lake invites you to look at it but the mirror of darkness prevents you seeing through it, so love's mysterious ground in God's love prevents you from seeing its source. (Kierkegaard 1964: 27)

This 'negative theology' is Kierkegaard's dialectical gesture of *wink*: the invisible, which is the origin of all that is visible, refuses to pass through the prism of *logos*. It is Pseudo-Dionysus's 'dazzling darkness' (Pseudo-Dionysus 1988: 133–42): here 'the path of light changes to darkness when one turns toward the light' (Kierkegaard 1964: 26). The heart of Love – Love himself – from where all commandment of love flows mysteriously is the invisible. As such, love is Life itself, life *as* life – Life as the invisible origin of all creaturely life – life that is released from the captures of the law, the messianic life: 'The life of love has an eternal spring' (ibid.: 27).

This life is the invisible. No speculative-dialectical phenomenology can render it visible in the light of the day of world-history; it does not participate in the dialectical project of constituting the totality of the anonymous order of visibility. For Kierkegaard, 'secret' is this very dazzling darkness of life, the very life of faith. The life of love is the life of faith, faith that sees that which no eye sees: 'eye hath not seen, nor ear heard, neither have entered into the heart of man' (I Corinthians 2: 9). What no eye has seen and no ear heard, the eye of faith sees. Therefore, first comes – even before we speak of the love of the neighbour, and Kierkegaard insists on this and he begins his work precisely thus – that we *believe* in love, that we have faith in love, that we believe what is radically invisible.

> The first emphasis developed in these reflections was that one must believe in love; otherwise one will never become aware that it exists. But now we return again to the first point and say, repeating: believe in love! This is the first and last thing to be said about love if one is to know what love is ... therefore the last, the most blessed, the absolutely convincing evidence of love remains: love itself, which is known and recognized by the love in another. (Kierkegaard 1964: 32–3)

The invisibility of love in regard to knowledge, this non-presence of love in the work of the law, the radical surplus of love in regard to the economy of exchanges: if this excess of the infinite overflowing the finitude – which cannot be understood as the excess of 'ought' over 'is' – is the very idea of the ethical, and above all of what we can call 'indicative' ethics, then the fundamental attunement of Kierkegaardian thought can be called 'ethical' par excellence. Such infinity – 'eternity' is Kierkegaard's word – can only be *indicated*: one cannot deduce axiomatically acts as though from principles.

Such 'negative theology' – this insistence on the radical invisibility and incomprehensibility of Life – is, then, the very cornerstone of Kierkegaard's indicative ethics. Life does not serve as the *arché* or principle of the world. In this sense, what we call the 'indicative' ethics of Kierkegaard is similar to what Reiner Schürmann would call 'anarchic': not anarchic in the sense of a political doctrine or regime, but the tragic thought of being-without-*arché*, and thus without hegemonies (without 'why'). One does not found and ground – and thereby legitimise – worldly hegemonies from this invisible. The invisible does not serve here as 'principle' or *arché*; it is 'the dazzling darkness' or the *absconditus* which eschatologically singularises all that is *to come*; it welcomes the eschatological community to come: 'let us love one another'. This Johannine – and Kierkegaardian – mellowing down of the second commandment is not an axiomatic deduction from the first principle of the love of God: love here does not operate as the legitimising principle of any political hegemony.

The theocentric otherness does not exclude the social otherness, and the love of God does not shut the door of the solitary individual against the social other, but rather opens up the very possibility of the social otherness in love. Kierkegaard shows this by exhibiting the inextricable relation between the two commandments:

> Fundamentally love to God is decisive; from there arises love to one's neighbour. But the Christian love-command requires one to love God above all and then to love one's neighbour. In love and friendship preference is the middle term; in love to one's neighbour God is the middle term. Love God above all else and then love your neighbour and in your neighbour every man. Only by loving God above all else can one love his neighbour in the next human being. The next human being – he is one's neighbour – this the next human being in the sense that the next human being is every other human being. Understood in this way, the discourse was right when it stated at the beginning that if one loves his neighbour in a single other human being he loves all men. (Ibid.: 70)

That's why it is necessary, as one side of his *polemos*, to emphasise the irreducible singularity of the subjectivity: only when the subjectivity is released and absolved from the genus or species and from all abstract generality and totality can the ethical truly be posed as truly the *religious* problem par excellence. The individual first needs to be individual, that is, to be *individualised*: only as individual (that 'singular individual', as Kierkegaard repeats), released from particularity, can one be responsible-ethical subjectivity. And it is love of God that first of all *singularises* the self, the singular individual in utter abandonment and solitude, shorn of all worldly attributes and consolations. The love of God is born out of the 'dark night of the soul', and a new self too is born out of this loving, a loving from which a certain 'fear and trembling' is inseparable. Only such subjectivity can truly *respond*; that is: give a re-sponse to the call that *always already* has come to him/her, the call that – in a way – *always already* precedes him/her. Such is the truly immemorial call of love, erupting out of the depth of the invisible, summoning up the subjectivity to respond to: 'where art thou?'

Responding at the limit of knowledge – as if as it were out of non-knowledge – to the call that arrives from the invisible which can neither be anticipated by any phenomenological anticipation nor can it be thematised – for it exceeds all intelligibility of being – such responsible subjectivity can only be, for Kierkegaard, the subjectivity responding to faith. Kierkegaard presents such a responding subjectivity in the figure of Abraham in *Fear and Trembling* and understands it as the decisive subjectivity of decision in his *Concluding Unscientific Postscript*. Such a decision – the decision of faith itself, which is nothing other than response and responsibility – taken always at the limit of knowledge, out of non-knowledge as it were, occurs when the normative-prescriptive order of moral law gets suspended. One cannot thus justify, and Kierkegaard does not justify either, Abraham's decision. Understood normatively-prescriptively, Abraham's decision remains infanticide, an unforgivable criminal act.

Given the radical invisibility – the radical secret of life – which refuses to be embodied in the statements of universal communicability and of normative-prescriptive moral law, the ethical here can only be indicative; in other words, it must pass through the negative gestures of eschatological suspension, indicating a *singularisation to come*. This 'singularisation to come' Kierkegaard calls *becoming*, and he rigorously distinguishes this from the Hegelian speculative concept of becoming. Only the *spirit* becomes, and spirit, for Kierkegaard, is only the spirit of faith: the radical decision is always the decision of the spirit; it is always the spiritual decision, the decision of faith, and only out of the decision that responsible subjectivity comes-to-be, that is, it *becomes*. So, 'you *shall* love', imperative though it is, cannot be a prescriptive-normative law that can be codified in a system of knowledge; what is needed rather is an existential transformation, a *becoming* of the spirit, a *tearing* of the selfish-narcissistic, blind love that sees only the immediately visible and knowable. For whoever sees only the visible is blind: this is the meaning of the Narcissus story who sees only the visible, that is, only oneself. To see only oneself is to be blind. To see the other who is secret – and the wholly other who is invisible – is to see with the eyes of faith, that is, first of all, to believe in love itself. In this rigorous sense, Narcissus's love – which is not tempered with the eternal and which is not transformed from the erotic self-love into the love of the neighbour – is not truly love: this struggle between love and love is the fundamental idea of Kierkegaard's *Works of Love*.

Such an indicative ethics cannot present itself as a philosophical discipline, nor can the writer – namely, Kierkegaard, who now signs his own work – present himself as an 'authority'. As Christian *reflection*, *Works of Love* is to be distinguished from Christian *sermons*. The Christian sermon operates through authority; it presupposes the authority of the holy writ and of Christ's apostles. The Christian reflection, on the other hand, does not presuppose authority. Kierkegaard, thus, *reflects* on love without authority. As a layman without authority (the word *Laos* meaning people called by God), Kierkegaard here does not prescribe universal, moral principles for everyone in order to solicit from them a normative obligation as to a hegemonic authority in place. A Christian reflection without authority would rather be a 'gadfly' – such is the indicative nature of the ethical – which makes the reader restless, tearing her or his self out of the comfort of its closure, exposing her or him open to the exhortation by which eternity transforms the finite and the earthly: 'you *shall* love'. The one who hears this address, the one who is addressed directly as 'you' here, is not a member of a genus to which s/he belongs as a biological-natural determinant entity; s/he is not a qualitatively indifferential entity belonging to a historical-political regime called the state: s/he is rather the 'single individual', each one alone an ecstatic-restless *existent* who hears the commandment: 'you shall love your neighbour as you love yourself'.

Critique of politics

Such an indicative ethics that operates without authority – an ethics that exhorts *each one* singularly *oneself* to be the neighbour of the one who is *the first to come by* – such an indicative ethics puts into question any attempt at totalisation of politics. The fundamental presupposition of Kierkegaardian ethics is this: that politics is not total and is not everything. If Kierkegaard is to be called a 'political theologian', it is in this decisive anti-Schmittean sense. Against Carl Schmitt who makes the distinction between friend and enemy as the very constitutive of the concept of the political, the political theologian Kierkegaard would break away all distinction between friend and enemy in the neighbour-love:

> therefore he who in truth loves his neighbour loves also his enemy. The distinction *friend or enemy* is a distinction in the object of love, but the object of love in one's neighbour is without distinction. One's neighbour is the absolutely unrecognizable distinction between man and man; it is eternal equality before God – enemies, too, have this equality. (Kierkegaard 1964: 79)

This is because 'erotic love is determined by the object', while 'only love to one's neighbour is determined by love'; in this rigorous, Christian sense, neighbour-love is decisively true love, because 'its object is without any of the more definite qualifications of difference, which means that this love is recognizable only by love' (ibid.: 77).

If the distinction between friend and enemy is very constitutive of politics as such – as Carl Schmitt understands it (Schmitt 2007) – then the neighbour-love puts a limit to all politics. 'You shall love your neighbour as yourself' cannot be part of a political programme; it is not a project of any calculable politics of practical, conditioned negotiations. There is, thus, indeed *obligation* to love one's neighbour, but this unconditional and non-negotiable obligation cannot be enforced by any given world-historical hegemonic power in place. In that sense, this obligation is *spiritual* par excellence. The *spirit* here means freedom from any normative obligation to the world-political regime in place. The spiritual love releases us from any natural ties of life that are biologically-racially determined and places us in radical freedom. 'Neighbour is the unqualified category of spirit' (Kierkegaard 1964: 79):

> Spiritual love, on the other hand, takes away from myself all natural determinants and all self-love. Therefore love for my neighbour cannot make me one with the neighbour in a united self. Love to one's neighbour is love between two individual beings, each eternally qualified as spirit. Love to one's neighbour is spiritual love, but two spirits are never able to become a single self in a selfish way. (Ibid.: 68–9)[1]

Here all mythic foundation of community where (naturally determinant) particular individuals get fused into a homogenous unity is interrupted. The spiritual community is a *new* community. It is not the community where many 'I' get fused into some naturally determined identity – a bigger 'I'.

The spirit interrupts all the mythic unity. Understood in a deeper way, 'flesh' – in opposition to spirit – in Christian thought does not mean sensuous or bodily; hence the Christian idea of spirit is not opposed to the bodily or sensuousness; it is rather opposed to the selfishness of sensuality which it calls 'flesh': 'sensuality, the flesh, Christianity understands as selfishness ... therefore self-love, egocentricity, is sensuality' (ibid.: 65). The Christian equality of the neighbour-love, then, is to be distinguished from the quantitative equality which historical-political regimes try to establish in the profane order:

> Earthly likeness, if it was possible, is not Christian equality. And perfect achievement of earthly likeness is an impossibility. Well-meaning worldliness really confesses this itself. It rejoices when it succeeds in making temporal conditions similar for more and more, but it recognises that its struggle is a pious wish, that it has taken on an enormous task, that it prospects are remote – if it rightly understood itself it would perceive that its vision will never be achieved in time, that even if this struggle were continued for millennia it would never attain its goal. Christianity, on the other hand, aided by the short-cut of the eternal, is immediately at the goal: it allows all distinctions to stand, but it teaches the equality of the eternal. It teaches that everyone shall *lift himself above* earthly distinctions. Notice carefully how equably it speaks. It does not say that it is the poor who shall lift themselves above earthly distinctions, while the mighty should perhaps come down from their elevation – ah, no, such talk is not equable, and the likeness which is obtained by the mighty climbing down and the poor climbing up is not Christian equality; this is the worldly likeness. No, if one stands at the top, even if one is the king, he shall *lift himself above* the distinction of his high position, and the beggar shall *lift himself above* the distinction of his poverty. Christianity lets all the distinctions of earthly existence stand, but in the command of love, in loving one's neighbour, this equality of lifting oneself above the distinctions of earthly existence is implicit. (Ibid.: 82–3)

As an 'anticommunist manifesto' (Löwith 1991: 114), Kierkegaard makes the qualitative distinction between the ethical-Christian 'equality of eternity' and the quantitative 'worldly likeness' that one achieves over a long, long time; a distinction co-relative to the Kierkegaardian qualitative dialectical disjunction between the qualitative eternity and the quantitative endless temporal movement on the homogenous plan of profane history: the latter only approximates but never achieves eternity, for it pushes eternity to an ever-remote distant *telos*. Franz Rosenzweig transforms this Kierkegaardian eschatological critique of world-historical time as qualitatively indifferent and provisional into his own messianic critique of world-historical politics.[2] Rising against the 'worshipper of progress' – namely, those worshipers of world-historical politics who believe in the 'ideal goal' set against the horizon of indefinite lengthening of time – Rosenzweig affirms the arrival of Messiah that can happen today, in the immediate future where the furthest distance can be expected in the nearest:[3]

> where the Kingdom advances in the world with unforeseeable steps and where every moment must be ready to receive the plenitude of eternity, the furthest distance is that which is expected at the nearest moment, and so

that which is nearest, that which is only the placeholder of the furthest, of the highest, of the whole, becomes accessible at every moment. (Ibid.: 245)

For Kierkegaard, radical equality between humans can never be achieved by a conditioned means of programmatic world-politics, and with regard to a parameter which is temporal and forever provisional; only by a measure which exceeds all conditions and closures, and consequently exceeds measure itself – namely, eternity, the measureless eternity – can all earthly distinctions be overcome: 'by the short-cut of the eternal and is immediately at the goal'. But this measureless eternity can never be found in the immanent plane of conditioned world-historical politics, for all world-historical politics violently subsumes singular beings under the 'maximising thrust of the universal', under genus and species.

> Just so high has Christianity set every man, absolutely every human being – because before Christ just as in the sight of God there is no aggregate, no mass; the innumerable are for him numbered – they are unmitigated individuals. Just so high has Christianity placed every man in order that he should not damage his soul by preening himself over or grovelling under the differences in earthly existence. (Kierkegaard 1964: 80)

The indicative ethics of neighbourly love, then, is always in dissymmetry and heterogeneity – 'out of joint' with the conditioned, pragmatic worldly-politics:

> Love to one's neighbour has the perfection of the eternal – *this is perhaps why at times it seems to fit in so imperfectly with earthly relationships and with earthly temporal distinctions, why it is easily misunderstood and exposed to hate, and why in any case it is very thankless to love one's neighbour.* (Ibid.; Kierkegaard's italics)

The *non-contemporaneity* between the neighbour-love and all other earthly relations takes away from all inter-human relations the character of absoluteness and autochthony: 'but *the highest* has never quite fitted into the relationships of earthly life – it is *both too little and too much*' (ibid.: 95; Kierkegaard's italics). This *non-contemporaneity, out of sync* with all worldly relations, is essentially that of the *surplus* of ethics of love over politics. This understanding of the other – who is each time *my* neighbour, that is, s/he who is free and is absolved from genus or species – is closer to Lévinas's messianic ethics of justice than Lévinas perhaps would like to allow himself to admit. The crucial question here is to emphasise their respective critiques of totality, whether that critique operates in the name of infinity or eternity, in the name of justice or of love, whether it is in a Jewish messianic manner or in a Christian eschatological manner. In each case, the ethical always operates as response and responsibility, infinite and unconditional, to the other who is every bit other, the whole humanity in each face: 'with your neighbour you have before God the equality of humanity' (ibid.: 72). Kierkegaard writes:

> He is your neighbour on the basis of equality with you before God; but this equality absolutely every man has, and he has it absolutely. (Ibid.)

This could have been written equally by Lévinas. However, in the proximity between what I call Kierkegaard's indicative ethics and Lévinas's ethics as first philosophy, there lies an irreducible distance: the very place of God. At a distance from Lévinas's God who comes to mind in the face of the other (hu)man, Kierkegaard makes the neighbourly love – the love of the other – as that which follows from the love of God. Even before we love each other, it is God who loves us first, and we are what we are, responses to the first, immemorial call of love coming from an invisible origin. As such, the neighbour-love, for Kierkegaard, is the in-between humans – the third or the middle[4] – which makes, first of all, sociality at all possible: 'worldly wisdom thinks that love is a relationship between man and man. Christianity teaches that love is a relation between: man-God-man, that is, that God is the middle term' (ibid.: 112–13). God is not the result of human sociality: this will be something like paganism for Kierkegaard, if not atheism. As the invisible origin of human love and as the immeasurable parameter that transfigures the inter-human love into eternity, God is not just the face of the neighbour; it is rather in the light of divine love that it is possible to bestow upon neighbourly love the seal of eternity; otherwise, we won't have the parameter of the unconditional to distinguish the neighbourly love from all inter-human relation and earthly distinctions. This makes Kierkegaard's ethics of sociality an irreducibly theocentric one, as distinguished from Lévinas's ethics of sociality where the place of God is being transformed into the place for the neighbour. The relationship between Kierkegaard and Lévinas becomes sharper when we take into account Jacques Derrida's critical reading of Lévinas (Derrida 1978: 79–195). Like Lévinas, Derrida understands the unconditional ethical responsibility as that which surpasses politics: in this sense Derrida is closer to Lévinasian messianic ethics than perhaps to Kierkegaard's Christian eschatological ethics of indication. However, the 'entre nous' – between the two of us – needs to be opened up to the third in order to think of infinity of the ethical without closure, a suggestion which Lévinas gracefully acknowledges in his later works. Kierkegaard works out the place of the middle – the third, the in-between – in his own singular, Christocentric way, a gesture that perhaps makes him, compared to the early Lévinas, closer to Derrida's thought in still another way.

Who is *my* neighbour?

> Who, then, is one's neighbour? The word is clearly derived from *neahgebur* [near-dweller]; consequently your neighbour is he who dwells nearer than anyone else, yet not in the sense of partiality, for to love him who through favouritism is nearer to you than all others is self-love – 'Do not the heathens also do the same?' Your neighbour, then, is nearer to you than all others ... if there are only two people, the other person is the neighbour. If there are millions, everyone of these is one's neighbour, that is, again, one who is closer than *the friend* and *the beloved*, inasmuch 7as these, as objects of partiality, lie so close to one's self-love. (Kierkegaard 1964: 37–8)[5]

The other calls me to an absolutely unconditional response and responsibility that tears away all my egoistic-narcissist love. The self has to lose and renounce all its selfishness, all the violence that erupts from its selfishness, and give up all the attributes of its power – and, thus, come to be truly self, the new self, the self of responsibility – in order to respond truly as responsible subjectivity. Thus, responsibility is first of all made possible not out of the power of the self over the other, nor on the basis of its force of appropriation, but out of the original renunciation of its selfishness. The self is truly self – the self of responsibility – when the self is not selfish.

It is true that unlike Kierkegaard who understands the neighbour as 'thou' ('one's neighbour is the first-thou' (Kierkegaard 1964: 69)), Lévinas understands the other as the 'he' – the third person – so as to break from all symmetry that may exist between I and thou. Against Martin Buber's dialogic-existential philosophy, Lévinas proposes the irreducible height from which the other addresses 'me' to my irrevocable responsibility, holding *me* hostage, as it were, by the weakness of his or her gaze. Kierkegaard, on the other hand, preserves the *He* only for God who is absolutely Other with regard to which the neighbour-love between self and other human can only be understood as a 'I-thou'. However, with regard to all erotic love which is constituted symmetrically (between I and the other I), the neighbour-love breaks away from all symmetry and synchrony: in this sense, the neighbour is truly and radically a 'thou', while the other of all partial, erotic love is just another 'I'.

This is how the eternity of the neighbourly love interrupts and disrupts all my subterfuges, all my cunning attempts to return to myself in the circular return to the same. The neighbour is the other who breaks the circle of self-love which operates in manifold disguises in all earthly and erotic love, and in all our normative allegiances – to the nation and to state, to the racially determined community and to the biologically determined family. So, the question (who is *my* neighbour?) ultimately turns to *me* and becomes a question concerning *me* as the neighbour: I *am* the neighbour to the other, to all others, to every other human being. Referring to the New Testament parable of the good Samaritan, Kierkegaard shows how the inversion of the question leads to the deeper meaning of the question asked:

> If anyone with this view asks, 'Who is my neighbour?' then Christ's reply to the Pharisee contains the answer only in singular way, for in the answer the question is first turned around to mean essentially: in what manner is one to ask the question? After having told the parable of the merciful Samaritan (Luke 10: 36), Christ says to the Pharisee, 'Which of these three, do you think, proved neighbour to the man who fell among the robbers?' the Pharisee answers correctly, 'The one who showed mercy on him'. This means that by recognising your duty you easily discover who your neighbour is. The Pharisee's answer is contained in Christ's question, which by its form necessitated the Pharisee's answering in this way. He towards whom I have a duty is my neighbour, and when I fulfil my duty I prove that I am a neighbour. Christ does not speak about recognising one's neighbour but about being a neighbour oneself, about proving oneself to be a neighbour, something the Samaritan showed by his compassion. By this he did not prove that the assaulted man was his neighbour but that he was a neighbour of the one assaulted. The Levite and the priest were in a stricter sense neighbours of the assaulted man, but they wished to ignore it. One the other hand, the Samaritan, who because of prejudice was destined to misunderstanding, nevertheless understood rightly that he was a neighbour of the assaulted man. (Ibid.: 38–9)

Again, in more in proximity to Lévinas, the question of neighbour-love, of response and responsibility, is turned towards 'me': it's *me*, not another, *me* before anyone else who must love the other, without all economy of mutuality and exchange, without all symmetry of erotic love, without the conditionality of all negotiations and values. Even more than erotic love, the neighbour-love is a gift which, unlike erotic love, is not based upon fortune but on an infinite task that the self, freed from all normative obligations, must assume, not because the faculty of practical reason asks one to, but in the face of God who has become man and who died on the cross. Thus, the response to the question, 'who is *my* neighbour': it is *me* who is *accentuated*, that is, I am the neighbour to the other who is nearer to me than anyone else, and this nearness to *me* absolutely everyone has.

The law of love

'Love your neighbour': if this law is not to be understood as a normative obligation to any law of the world-political regime in place and to any *nomos* of the earth, how then is this law in relation to the neighbour-love to be understood? For, it appears that law by definition is opposed to love, as death is to life. As Kierkegaard brings out this fundamental contradiction at the very heart of Christian love:

> Under the law man groans. Wherever he looks he sees only demands, never a boundary – like one who looks out over the ocean and sees wave after wave, but never a boundary. Wherever he looks he meets only severity, which in its infinitude can always become more severe, never the boundary where it becomes mildness. The law strikes us out, as it were; one never gets his fill by its help, for its character is precisely to take away, to demand, to exact to the uttermost, and the continuous regression of indefiniteness in the multiplicity of all its provisions constitutes an inexorable collection-statement of demands. With every provision the law demands something, and yet there is no limit to the provisions. The law is therefore the very contradiction of life, but life is fulfilment. The law resembles death. (Ibid.: 111–12)

The Christian ethics of the sociality of love must respond to this fundamental contradiction at the heart of love itself: on the one hand, 'Christ is the end of the law' (Romans 10: 4), and yet, on the other hand, 'love is the fulfilling of the law' (Romans 13: 10). Both come from the mouth of the same apostle, St Paul. If Christ – who is Love Himself – is the end of the law, the arrival of Christ is supposed to mean abolition or suspension of the law: love here is in decisive conflict with the law. Instead of fulfilling the law, Paul appears to speak here about the abolition of the law. Kierkegaard remarks on Paul:

> 'Christ is the end of the law'. What the law was unable to produce – as little as it could save a man – that Christ was. Whereas the law with its demand thereby became the destruction of all, because they were not what it demanded and only learned to recognise sin through it, Christ became the law's destruction because he was what it demanded. (Kierkegaard 1964: 106)

However, Kierkegaard proposes a deeper understanding of this contradiction. Thought of rigorously, this apparent contradiction points itself towards a deeper truth about love itself:

> its destruction, its consummation – for when the demand is fulfilled, the demand exists only in the fulfilment, but consequently it does not exist as a demand. Just as thirst when it is satisfied exists only in the solace of refreshment, so Christ came not to abolish the law but to fulfil it; therefore from that time on it exists in the perfect fulfilment. (Ibid.)

This does not mean, simply understood, that there is opposition as such between the law and love; it is rather that *in* love this opposition does not exist; here 'end' and 'fulfilment' opens itself to the other: 'law requires and love gives' (ibid.: 112).

If there is no decisive conflict between the law and love, does this mean that Kierkegaard's ethics of sociality finally turns out to be an apology of the world? It would be so if by the law Kierkegaard here means nothing other than the *nomos* of the worldly existence, as if Christ's love is the fulfilment of the *nomos* of the worldly existence. 'Love thy neighbour': this is neither the worldly love nor the worldly law. In this commandment, love rather comes up against the law of the worldly, and turns out to be the criticism of the world. Therefore, here the collision is not between the law and love per se, but between the worldly love and neighbour-love, and between the worldly *nomos* and the divine commandment. The truth at stake here is the very *truth* of Christianity which is a scandal for the Jews and foolishness for the Greeks, the truth whose offensive character the 1,800 years of Christendom happily covers over, and harmonises it with the worldly truth by aesthetising, deifying, glorifying and reifying the world. Understood in the apostolic spirit, love is the criticism of the world. That is why Kierkegaard could say that Christ's

> Whole life was a terrible collision with the merely human conception of what love is. It was the ungodly world which crucified him, but even his disciples did not understand him and continuously sought, so it seemed, to win him to their idea of what love is, so that once he had to say to Peter, 'Get behind me, Satan'. (Ibid.: 115)

Christ's crucifixion is love's judgement upon the *nomos* of the world. Without this unconditional love coming from God – which can only come from God, such is the mystery of divine love! – love can only be mutual agreement between humans, a 'merely human judgement'. Such love 'thereby escapes the possibility of the horror of the ultimate and most terrible collision: that in the love relationship there is an infinite difference between the conceptions of what love is' (ibid.: 118). So, the Kierkegaardian heterogeneity that qualifies his dialectics as qualitative lies in the different conceptions of love. It is the heterogeneity or the dissymmetry between the love that is unconditional, which for that matter exceeds all economy, of return and profit, of all exchanges, and even of the economy of sacrifice, and, on the other hand, the love that makes even sacrifice a matter of economic return. The love of God and, consequently, the neighbour-love, is sacrificial love where the economy of the worldly love is sacrifice, without reward:

> God, on the other hand, understands love to be sacrificing love, sacrificing love in a divine sense, love which sacrifices everything in order to make room for God, even if a heavy sacrifice were to become still heavier because no one understands it, which in yet another sense belongs to true sacrifice. The sacrifice which is understood by men has its reward in the approval of

men and to that extent is no true sacrifice, for a true sacrifice must unconditionally be without reward. (Ibid.: 123)

Such is the law of love which has within it its double presupposition: on one hand such sacrificial love is qualitatively heterogeneous to the *nomos* of the world, on the other hand such love is mutually related to the law, divinely understood, when the law is understood as commandment.

In the eyes of the world-historical politics that is irreversibly marching ahead in triumph, celebrating worldly success and enjoyment of the worldly goods, the sacrificial love of the crucified God appears to be madness, and every work of neighbour-love looks like foolishness and a scandal. Yet, without this madness and offence of sacrificial love, there is neither the rigour of the ethical to be found nor the sense of the political to be understood. The truth of Kierkegaard's sociality of love lies in this offence that love begets, and his *polemos* is aimed precisely in wounding us with this thorn in our flesh: that persecuted truth, which is the only truth, is not the truth of the world:

> But to stand on the elevated peak (for sacrifice is truly elevation) criticized, despised, hated, mocked almost worse than the most base among the debased – consequently, superhumanly striving to attain the elevated point and to stand on the elevation in such a way that it appears to all as if one stood at the lowest point of contempt – this, Christianly understood, is sacrifice, and it is also, humanly understood, madness ... Christianly understood, this is what it is to love. If it is true that to love is the greatest happiness, this is the heaviest suffering – if it were not that being related to God is the greatest blessedness. (Ibid.: 133–4)

Notes

1. Kierkegaard goes on to say: 'only in love to one's neighbour is the self, which loves, spiritually qualified simply as spirit and has neighbour as purely spiritual' (Kierkegaard 1964: 69).
2. Thus, Rosenzweig could say: 'Eternity is not a very long time, but a tomorrow that just as well could be today. Eternity is a future, which, without ceasing to be future, is nevertheless present. Eternity is a today that would be conscious of being more than today' (Rosenzweig 2005: 241).
3. Rosenzweig writes: 'This is almost the *shibboleth* by which one can tell the believer in the Kingdom from the true worshipper of progress: whether he does not defend himself in the next moment against the perspective and duty of anticipating the "goal". Without this anticipation and the inner pressure to realize it, without "the desire to make the Messiah arrive before his time" and the attempt "to do violence to the heavenly Kingdom", the future is not a future, but only a past drawn out to an infinite length, past projected forward. For, without this anticipation, the moment is not eternal but something that interminably crawls along the long strategic roadway of time' (Rosenzweig 2005: 244).
4. Kierkegaard says: 'nevertheless neighbour is definitely the middle term of self-renunciation which steps in between self-love's I and I and also comes between erotic love's and friendship's I and the other I' (Kierkegaard 1964: 66–7).

5. Similarly, Rosenzweig writes: 'the commandment designates this something as the neighbour, and of course, both in holy language and in Greek, the word means the neighbour at the precise moment of love; it matters little what he was before this moment of love and what he will be afterwards, in any case, at this moment, he is only the neighbour for me. The neighbour is therefore only a representative; he is not loved for himself, he is not loved for his beautiful eyes, but only because he is just there, because he is just my neighbour. In his place – in this place that is for me the one neighbouring on me – there could just well be another person; the neighbour is the other, the *plesios* of the Septuagint, the *plesios allos* of Homer' (Rosenzweig 2005: 234).

Bibliography

Adorno, Theodor, *Negative Dialectics*, trans. E. B. Ashton (London and New York: Bloomsbury Academic, 1981).
Adorno, Theodor and Max Horkheimer, *Dialectic of Enlightenment: Philosophical Fragments*, trans. Edmund Jephcott (Stanford: Stanford University Press, 2002).
Angelus Silesius, *Cherubinic Wanderer*, trans. Maria Shrady (Mahwah, NJ: Paulist Press, 1986).
Benjamin, Walter, *Illuminations*, ed. Hannah Arendt and trans. Harry Zohn (New York: Schocken Books, 1985).
Benjamin, Walter, *Reflections*, ed. Peter Demetz (New York: Schocken Press, 1986).
Bensussan, Gerard, *Marx le Sortant* (Paris: Hermann, 2007).
Bloch, Ernst, *The Spirit of Utopia*, trans. Anthony Nassar (Stanford: Stanford University Press, 2000).
Bloch, Ernst, *Atheism in Christianity: The Religion of the Exodus and the Kingdom*, trans. Peter Thomson (London: Verso, 2009).
Bonhoeffer, Dietrich, *The Cost of Discipleship*, trans. R. H. Fuller (New York: SCM Press, 1995).
Breton, Stanislas, *A Radical Philosophy of Saint Paul*, trans. Joseph N. Ballan with an Introduction by Ward Blanton (New York: Columbia University Press, 2011).
Derrida, Jacques, 'Violence and Metaphysics: An Essay on the Thought of Emmanuel Levinas' in *Writing and Difference*, trans. Alan Bass (Chicago: University of Chicago Press, 1978), pp. 79–195.
Derrida, Jacques, 'Différance' in *Margins – of Philosophy*, trans. Alan Bass (Chicago: Chicago University Press, 1984), pp. 1–28.
Derrida, Jacques, *The Gift of Death*, trans. David Wills (Chicago and London: The University of Chicago Press, 1992a).
Derrida, Jacques, *Given Time: I. Counterfeit Money*, trans. Peggy Kamuf (Chicago: University of Chicago Press, 1992b).
Frank, Manfred, *Der Unendliche Mangel an Sein: Schellings Hegelkritik und die Anfange der Marxschen Dialektik* (Frankfurt: Suhrkamp, 1975).
Habermas, Jürgen, 'Ernst Bloch: A Marxist Schelling' in *Philosophical-Political Profiles*, trans. Frederick G. Lawrence (Cambridge, MA and London: The MIT Press, 1985), pp. 61–78.
Hegel, G. W. F., *Lectures on the Philosophy of History*, trans. J. Sibree (London: G. Bells & Sons, 1900).

Hegel, G. W. F., *Phenomenology of Spirit*, trans. A. V. Miller (Oxford: Oxford University Press, 1977).
Hegel, G. W. F., *Faith and Knowledge*, trans. Walter Cerf and H. S. Harris (Albany: State University of New York Press, 1988).
Heidegger, Martin, *Schelling's Treatise on the Essence of Human Freedom*, trans. Joan Stambaugh (Athens: Ohio University Press, 1985).
Heidegger, Martin, *The Question Concerning Technology and Other Essays*, trans. William Levitt (New York: Harper Torchbooks, 1997).
Heidegger, Martin, 'On the Essence of Ground' in *Pathmarks*, ed. William McNeill (Cambridge, MA: Cambridge University Press, 1998).
Hengel, Martin, *Crucifixion* (Philadelphia: Fortress Press, 1977).
Henry, Michel, *I am the Truth: Toward a Philosophy of Christianity*, trans. Susan Emanuel (Stanford: Stanford University Press, 2002).
Hölderlin, Friedrich, *Poems and Fragments*, trans. Michael Hamburger (London: Routledge & Kegan Paul, 1966).
John of the Cross, *The Collected Works of Saint John of the Cross*, trans. Kieran Kavanaugh and Otilio Rodriguez (Washington, DC: ICS Publications, 1991).
Jonas, Hans, *The Imperative of Responsibility: In Search of an Ethics for the Technological Age* (Chicago: University of Chicago Press, 1985).
Jüngel, Eberhard, '"You Talk like a Book . . .": Toward an Understanding of the Philosophical Fragments of J. Climacus' in *Theological Essays*, trans. Arnold Neufeldt-Fast and J. B. Webster (London and New York: Bloomsbury, 2014).
Kant, Immanuel, 'An Answer to the Question: "What is Enlightenment"' in *Political Writings*, ed. H. S. Reiss (Cambridge: Cambridge University Press, 1991), pp. 54–60.
Kierkegaard, Søren, *Journals or Papirer*, vols I–XI (København: Glydendalske Boghandel, 1909–1948).
Kierkegaard, Søren, *The Concept of Dread*, trans. Walter Lowrie (Princeton: Princeton University Press, 1957).
Kierkegaard, Søren, *Works of Love*, ed. and trans. Howard Hong and Edna Hong (New York: Harper & Row, 1964).
Kierkegaard, Søren, *Attack upon "Christendom"*, trans. Walter Lowrie (Princeton: Princeton University Press, 1968).
Kierkegaard, Søren, *Christian Discourses Etc.*, trans. Walter Lowrie (Princeton: Princeton University Press, 1971).
Kierkegaard, Søren, *For Self-Examination* and *Judge for Yourself*, trans. Howard Hong and Edna Hong (Princeton: Princeton University Press, 1991).
Kierkegaard, Søren, *Eighteen Upbuilding Discourses*, ed. and trans. Howard Hong and Edna Hong (Princeton: Princeton University Press, 1992).
Kierkegaard, Søren, *Fear and Trembling* and *The Book of Adler*, trans. Walter Lowrie (New York: Everyman's Library, 1994).
Kierkegaard, Søren, *Papers and Journals: A Selection*, trans. Alastair Hannay (London: Penguin Books, 1996).
Kierkegaard, Søren, *Training in Christianity*, trans. Walter Lowrie (New York: Vintage Classics, 2004).
Kierkegaard, Søren, *Repetition* and *Philosophical Fragments*, trans. M. G. Piety (Oxford: Oxford University Press, 2009a).
Kierkegaard, Søren, *Concluding Unscientific Postscript to the Philosophical Crumbs*, trans. Alastair Hannay (Cambridge: Cambridge University Press, 2009b).
Kierkegaard, Søren, *Two Ages: The Age of Revolution and the Present Age*, trans. Howard Hong and Edna Hong (Princeton: Princeton University Press, 2009c).
Kierkegaard, Søren, *Upbuilding Discourses in Various Spirits*, ed. and trans. Howard Hong and Edna Hong (Princeton: Princeton University Press, 2009d).
Kierkegaard, Søren, *Three Discourses on Imagined Occasions*, ed. and trans. Howard Hong and Edna Hong (Princeton: Princeton University Press, 2009e).

Kierkegaard, Søren, *The Present Age: On the Death of Rebellion*, trans. Walter Kaufmann (New York: Harper Perennial, 2010a).
Kierkegaard, Søren, *Spiritual Writings*, ed. and trans. George Pattison (New York: Harper Perennial, 2010b).
Lévinas, Emmanuel, *Totality and Infinity: An Essay on Exteriority*, trans. Alphonso Lingis (Pittsburgh: Duquesne University Press, 1969).
Lévinas, Emmanuel, 'Existence and Ethics' in *Kierkegaard: A Critical Reader*, ed. Jonathan Rée and Jane Chamberlain (Oxford: Wiley-Blackwell, 1998).
Löwith, Karl, *The Meaning in History: The Theological Implication of the Philosophy of History* (Chicago: Chicago University Press, 1957).
Löwith, Karl, *From Hegel to Nietzsche: The Revolution in Nineteenth Century Thought*, trans. David E. Green (New York: Columbia University Press, 1991).
McGrath, Sean, *The Dark Ground of Spirit: Schelling and the Unconscious* (New York: Routledge, 2012).
Meier, Heinrich, 'What is Political Theology?' in *Leo Strauss and the Theologico-Political Problem*, trans. Marcus Brainard (Cambridge: Cambridge University Press, 2006), pp. 75–88.
Moltmann, Jürgen, *The Coming of God: Christian Eschatology*, trans. Margaret Kohl (Minneapolis: Fortress Press, 2004).
Nietzsche, Friedrich, 'On the Uses and Disadvantages of History for Life' in *Untimely Meditations*, trans. R. J. Hollingdale (Cambridge: Cambridge University Press, 1997).
Peterson, Erik, 'Monotheism as a Political Problem' in *Theological Tractates*, trans. Michael J. Hollerich (Stanford: Stanford University Press, 2011), pp. 68–105.
Pseudo-Dionysus, 'The Mystical Theology' in *The Complete Works*, trans. Paul Rorem (New York: Paulist Press, 1988), pp. 133–42.
Rosenzweig, Franz, *The Star of Redemption*, trans. Barbara E. Galli (Wisconsin: University of Wisconsin Press, 2005).
Schelling, F. W. J. von, *Philosophical Inquiries into the Nature of Human Freedom*, trans. James Gutmann (La Salle: Open Court, 1936).
Schelling, F. W. J. von, *Idealism and the Endgame of Theory*, trans. Thomas Pfau (Albany: State University of New York Press, 1994).
Schelling, F. W. J. von, *The Grounding of Positive Philosophy*, trans. Bruce Matthews (Albany: State University of New York Press, 2007).
Schelling, F. W. J. von, *Philosophy and Religion*, trans. Klaus Ottmann (Putnam, CT: Spring Publications, 2010).
Schmitt, Carl, *Roman Catholicism and Political Form*, trans. G. L. Ulmen (New York: Greenwood Press, 1996).
Schmitt, Carl, *Political Theology: Four Chapters on the Concept of Sovereignty*, trans. George Schwab (Chicago and London: University of Chicago Press, 2005).
Schmitt, Carl, *The Nomos of the Earth: In the International Law of the Jus Publicum Europaeum*, trans. G. L. Ulmen (New York: Telos Press, 2006).
Schmitt, Carl, *The Concept of the Political*, trans. George Schwab (Chicago: University of Chicago Press, 2007).
Schmitt, Carl, *Political Theology II: The Myth of the Closure of Any Political Theology*, trans. Michael Hoelzl and Graham Ward (Cambridge: Polity Press, 2008a).
Schmitt, Carl, *Leviathan of the State Theory of Thomas Hobbes: Meaning and Failure of a Political Symbol*, trans. George Schwab and Erna Hilfstein (Chicago: University of Chicago Press, 2008b).
Scholem, Gershom, *Major Trends in Jewish Mysticism*, Foreword by Robert Alter (New York: Schocken Books, 1995).
Schürmann, Reiner, *Heidegger on Being and Acting: From Principles to Anarchy*, trans. Christine-Marie Gros (Bloomington: Indiana University Press, 1986).
Schürmann, Reiner, *Broken Hegemonies*, trans. Reginald Lilly (Bloomington: Indiana University Press, 2003).

Taubes, Jacob, *The Political Theology of Paul*, trans. Dana Hollander (Stanford: University Press, 2003).
Taubes, Jacob, *Occidental Eschatology*, trans. David Ratmoko (Stanford: Stanford University Press, 2009).
Taubes, Jacob, *To Carl Schmitt: Letters and Reflections*, trans. Keith Tribe with an Introduction by Mike Grimshaw (New York: Columbia University Press, 2013).

Names Index

Adorno, Theodor, 1, 35
Angelus Silesius, 24

Benjamin, Walter, 13, 35, 46, 104
Bensussan, Gerard, 23, 51
Bloch, Ernst, 21, 36
Blumenberg, Hans, 7, 23
Bonhoeffer, Dietrich, 46, 85
Breton, Stanislas, 26

Derrida, Jacques, 5, 71–3, 123

Eckhart, Meister, 23–4, 30

Frank, Manfred, 21

Habermas, Jürgen, 21
Hegel, G. W. F., 6, 8–12, 18, 20, 27, 29–30, 32–4, 36–7, 39–42, 44–5, 49, 53, 57–60, 62–3, 67, 75–6, 79, 82–4, 86, 88, 90–1, 93–4, 98, 107, 114–15
Heidegger, Martin, 2–3, 7, 23–4, 30, 36–7, 65
Hengel, Martin, 82
Henry, Michel, 80

Heraclitus, 13, 19
Hölderlin, Friedrich, 4, 13

Jonas, Hans, 3
Jünger, Eberhard, 52

Kant, Immanuel, 1, 113

Levinas, Emmanuel, 51, 55, 73, 110, 122–5
Löwith, Karl, 10–12, 20, 51, 75–6, 89, 91, 121

McGrath, Sean, 21
Marx, Karl, 19–21, 23, 33, 51, 75, 77, 89
Meier, Heinrich, 6
Moltmann, Jürgen, 4

Nietzsche, Friedrich, 19–21, 23, 37, 76–7, 83, 88–90, 92

Peterson, Erik, 14
Plotinus, 19, 25
Pseudo-Dionysus, 116

Rosenzweig, Franz, 21, 36, 51–2, 54, 61–2, 65, 88, 95–6, 121

Schelling, F. W. J. Von, 14–15, 17–33, 35–7, 41, 50, 61, 65, 95, 107
Schmitt, Carl, 6–10, 12–14, 19, 23, 72–3, 76, 93–4, 101, 108, 119–20
Scholem, Gershom, 25

Schürmann, Reiner, 3, 10, 23, 35, 40, 41, 46, 61, 89, 109, 117
Socrates, 19, 47, 49

Taubes, Jacob, 4, 7, 10, 13, 20–1, 93

Subject Index

abandonment, 14, 18, 24–5, 30, 31, 36–8, 54, 84–5, 118
Abfall, 25
Actuality, 7, 14, 17–18, 21–3, 25–6, 28–33, 36–7, 39–40, 45, 50, 53, 64–5, 89–90, 93, 95
analogia entis, 5–6, 9, 13–14, 24, 64, 101
arché, 1–4, 6, 10, 14–15, 23–4, 30, 33, 38, 44, 70, 89–90, 99, 117
auctoritus, 6–7, 9, 21, 93–4
Aufhebung, 2, 11, 42, 46
Ausgang, 18, 23, 51
authority, 7–9, 60, 89, 93–5, 99, 101, 113, 119

becoming, 2, 9, 12, 27, 38, 41–2, 44, 46, 48, 53, 58–61, 64, 66, 73, 76, 80, 82, 94, 99–100, 108, 111–12, 118
Begriff, 17, 28, 36, 38, 62

Christendom, 12, 14, 18, 19, 20, 61, 77–80, 82, 84–5, 87–9, 91, 94, 96, 99–104, 108–9, 127
Christianity, 11–12, 14, 17, 19, 20–1, 27, 33, 52–3, 59–61, 64, 66, 68, 76–82, 87–8, 96–104, 108–9, 120–3, 127
Church, 5, 11, 21, 26–8, 71, 77–82, 85, 92, 94, 103
concept, 5–7, 9, 11, 13–14, 17–18, 22, 28–9, 31–3, 35–41, 43–4, 47, 50, 52, 53–4, 56–9, 61–2, 68–9, 72–3, 76, 88, 91, 96, 100–1, 108, 110, 115, 118–19
conflagration, 4, 18, 31, 75, 96, 100

decision, 6–9, 12, 19–20, 31, 33, 41–3, 45, 47–8, 54, 57, 59–60, 65–6, 91–3, 118
dialectic, 1, 35–6, 38–44, 55–8, 60–4, 70, 78, 82, 88, 97–8, 100–1, 104, 107, 111, 113, 127

eschatology, 11, 14, 17–18, 20–2, 24, 50, 52, 57, 62, 75, 77, 80–1, 86, 88, 94–6, 98
eschaton, 3–4, 12, 31, 58, 94
eternity, 3, 12–13, 22, 42–4, 46, 48–9, 51–3, 58, 60, 79, 81, 83, 92, 94–5, 101, 103, 113, 115, 117, 119, 121–4
event, 3–6, 10–14, 17–18, 20–1, 24, 26–7, 30–3, 35–7, 40, 43–5, 47–8, 50, 52–4, 56–8, 62, 64–5, 68, 73, 76–7, 79, 85, 87–8, 91–2

exception, 4, 6–10, 12–14, 19, 23–5, 30, 33, 35–6, 45–6, 71, 92, 94–5
existence, 2, 8, 17–18, 20, 24, 26, 29, 31–3, 35–48, 50–2, 55–68, 70–1, 78–80, 87–8, 90–2, 99, 104, 111, 115–16, 121–2, 127

figura, 3
figuration, 3–5, 42, 76, 104

Gelassenheit, 18, 24, 37

Hegemonikon, 2, 15, 24, 36–8, 40, 89, 92
hegemony, 3–4, 14, 30, 33, 35, 39, 108, 117
history, 2, 4–6, 8–12, 14, 17–19, 21–3, 25–7, 31, 33, 37, 39–40, 44, 51–3, 55–8, 63, 66, 75–7, 79–81, 83–4, 86–8, 91, 93–4, 97–100, 103–4, 109, 112, 114–16, 121

Kairos, 46
Katechon, 9–10
kenosis, 4–5, 10, 14, 21, 23–4, 30–1, 36, 46, 49, 57, 64, 69, 81, 84, 98, 104
Koinon, 4, 23, 99, 109

idolatry, 61, 63–6, 68, 73, 97
immanence, 1–6, 8–9, 11–12, 14–15, 18, 20, 22–3, 29, 31, 36, 39, 42, 54, 64, 66–7, 73, 77, 89, 91, 93–5, 98, 103

law, 1–3, 5, 7–9, 13, 18–19, 23, 29, 31–2, 35–8, 41, 43–4, 46–8, 52, 55, 62, 66–9, 71–3, 85, 88, 90, 92, 95–7, 104, 107–9, 112–13, 116, 118, 125–8
life, 4, 7, 13, 20, 22, 24, 30, 35–7, 42–5, 47, 49, 50–2, 54, 56, 60–2, 64, 67–8, 70, 72–3, 76–83, 85–9, 92, 95–8, 101–2, 104, 113–14, 116–18, 120, 122, 126–7

love, 18–19, 24–6, 36, 47, 49–50, 55, 69, 72–3, 78, 82, 84–5, 95, 101, 103, 107–28

madness, 44, 54–5, 57, 61, 69, 115, 128
melancholy, 26, 42
moment, 3, 9, 13, 22, 38, 41–2, 44–53, 57, 59, 74, 86, 90, 92–3, 112–13, 121–2
mythic, 1–2, 5, 13, 24–5, 29–32, 35, 37–9, 43–4, 47, 49, 60, 62, 64, 66–7, 71, 73, 90–1, 94, 109, 120

negative, 1, 13–14, 18, 21–2, 28–30, 32–3, 35–6, 61–2, 66, 78, 107–8, 116–18
nomos, 1–2, 4–6, 9, 13, 23–4, 26, 78, 80, 92, 94, 126–8
nunc stans, 104

paradox, 1, 4–5, 7–8, 10, 12–13, 18–19, 22, 24, 31–2, 38, 43–52, 56–7, 59, 63–4, 66–71, 73, 78–80, 82–4, 86–9, 91, 94–5, 98, 104, 107–8, 114
phenomenology, 22, 26, 32, 44–5, 47, 49–50, 60, 90, 98, 116
pistis, 26, 80
pleroma, 31, 41–2, 47, 86
Pneuma, 72, 96, 98–9
political, 6–15, 17, 19–28, 30, 32–3, 42, 50–1, 54, 61–2, 64, 71–3, 75–6, 81, 90, 93–4, 96, 98, 100–1, 104, 107–10, 112, 114, 117, 119–21, 125, 128
potentiality, 2, 14, 17–19, 21–6, 28–31, 33, 36, 48, 50, 54, 65, 82

reason, 1–3, 6, 9–10, 12, 14, 20, 23–4, 27, 30, 39, 42–3, 49, 51, 53, 54, 57, 60–1, 69, 73–6, 80, 83, 86, 88–9, 98, 104, 113, 115, 125
redemption, 26, 41, 48, 50, 52, 61–2, 68, 86–9, 95–6

SUBJECT INDEX | 139

responsibility, 44, 55, 68, 70–2, 91–3, 110, 118, 122–4
revelation, 4, 19, 27, 32, 44, 46, 63–5, 71, 87–8

secularisation, 77
sovereignty, 3–4, 6–7, 9–10, 13–15, 17, 19, 21–7, 30, 33, 35, 45, 46, 50, 58, 66–7, 79, 84–5, 93, 95, 107–8
spacing, 37, 40, 42–5, 66, 91
speculative, 11, 32, 40–2, 44–5, 50–1, 54, 57, 60, 63, 66, 68, 75, 78–9, 82, 88, 90–1, 108, 115–16, 118
spirit, 12–14, 26, 31–2, 34, 38–9, 42, 44–7, 51, 55–6, 59–61, 63, 69, 72, 76, 78, 80, 86–8, 92, 96–9, 103–4, 109, 118, 120, 127
subject, 7, 15, 22–3, 32, 41–5, 49, 51, 55–6, 58–9, 61, 68–9, 72, 74, 101, 110–11, 114–15, 117–18, 124
system, 6–7, 9, 23, 27, 29, 31, 33, 37, 38, 58, 60, 63, 65–6, 84, 88, 90, 110–11, 118

theodicy, 5, 8, 12, 14, 17–23, 25, 31, 33, 56–8, 63, 67, 76–7, 79, 84, 86, 94, 98, 100, 103–4, 107
theology, 6, 8–14, 18–19, 21–2, 25, 28, 33, 43, 50, 54, 63, 76, 80–1, 93–4, 96, 101, 104, 107–9, 116–17
time, 3, 5–7, 9, 12–13, 20, 22–3, 36–7, 40, 42–9, 51–3, 57–63, 66, 70, 75–82, 86, 89, 92–3, 102–4, 110, 113, 115, 121–2, 126
transcendence, 2–6, 8, 10, 12, 14–15, 18, 20, 22–3, 25, 29, 36, 57–8, 62, 76, 93, 94

violence, 3, 13, 26–9, 31, 33, 35–9, 42–4, 47–8, 50–1, 54–5, 62, 67, 70–3, 76, 84, 86–8, 90, 92, 95–6, 104, 108, 112–15, 124

wink, 22, 114–16

EU representative:
Easy Access System Europe
Mustamäe tee 50, 10621 Tallinn, Estonia
Gpsr.requests@easproject.com

www.ingramcontent.com/pod-product-compliance
Lightning Source LLC
Chambersburg PA
CBHW070359240426
43671CB00013BA/2571